SPATIAL COMPUTING

SPATIAL
COMPUTING

AN AI-DRIVEN BUSINESS
REVOLUTION

CATHY HACKL   IRENA CRONIN

WILEY

For general information on our other products and services or for technical support, please contact our Customer Care Department within the United States at (800) 762-2974, outside the United States at (317) 572-3993 or fax (317) 572-4002.

Wiley also publishes its books in a variety of electronic formats. Some content that appears in print may not be available in electronic formats. For more information about Wiley products, visit our web site at www.wiley.com.

Library of Congress Cataloging-in-Publication Data is Available:

ISBN 9781394244416 (Cloth)
ISBN 9781394244423 (ePub)
ISBN 9781394244430 (ePDF)

Cover design: Wiley
Cover Image: © wacomka / Adobe Stock
Author Photos: Courtesy of the Authors
SKY10070732_032424

Cathy Hackl

I dedicate this book to my dad, Ambassador Luis Varela, the man who taught me to have a rebellious soul, a voracious appetite for learning, and the heart of an explorer. Te amo con todo mi alma papito bello!

I also dedicate this book to all the women working in Spatial Computing, AI, XR, and tech in general. We can change the future by making technology better!

Irena Cronin

For the memory of my husband, Danny, and his love of tech.

Contents

FOREWORD

The Inception of Our New Spatial Reality: Immerse or Die!

Apple had its next iPhone moment with the launch of its Vision Pro in 2024. Like in 2007, Apple yet again shifted the trajectory of computing behaviors by developing an intelligent and immersive Spatial Computing platform. And like in 2007, the world will never be the same. An entirely new operating system unlocked entirely new dimensions. These infinite, layered canvases bestowed users with metahuman capabilities. Now, people in any context can interact with information, content, and each other in ways and in spaces that didn't exist in traditional physical and digital realms. We thus gain access to unprecedented worlds and experiences with unimagined worlds forming in virtual and augmented realms every day.

But wait, there's more. Eight or so months before the introduction of Apple's Vision Pro, OpenAI released ChatGPT, introducing generative AI to the masses. In fact, ChatGPT is widely regarded as the fastest-growing consumer internet app of all time, reaching an estimated 100 million monthly users in just two months.[1] Generative AI is also in its own way giving users superpowers by augmenting their efforts with Artificial Intelligence. In fact, most apps and platforms will automatically integrate generative AI as parts of its user interface (UI). It will just seamlessly blend in to digital experiences. Added to Spatial Computing, AI-powered experiences supercharge human potential by arming them with a cognitive exoskeleton, augmented and virtual vision, and the ability to interact with computers, robots, data, and one another in three-dimensional other-worldly spaces.

And that's where this story begins.

Humans are now entering into uncharted portals of hybrid realities that are not only intelligent and immersive, but also transcendent. They augment human capabilities to unlock exponential performance and previously unattainable outcomes in evolving hybrid dimensions that foster the intermundane relationship between physical and digital worlds.

Cathy Hackl and Irena Cronin are about to deliver a transformative inception by planting the idea of spatial innovation to spark your imagination to create new worlds, new ways of working, new ways of learning, new ways of communicating, new ways of exploring, and new ways of dreaming, remembering, inventing, solving, and evolving.

This frontier between the physical and digital world will be shaped by you and fellow readers. You are the architects of these unexplored worlds. You are the astronomers who discover them. You are the pioneers who explore these new territories. And it's your vision that defines the next chapter of spatial design, experiences, and human potential.

What a *virtual* world we now live in!

Immerse or die!

Brian Solis

Digital Futurist, Anthropologist, 9x Best-Selling Author, Metahuman,
briansolis.com

INTRODUCTION

The Converging Frontiers of AI and Spatial Computing

A pivotal moment is at the heart of this discussion; one that will reshape our world as we know it. This convergence embodies the union of two potent forces: Artificial Intelligence (AI) and Spatial Computing, epitomized by Augmented Reality (AR) and Virtual Reality (VR). This fusion represents an intricate dance between innovation and creativity, offering a novel lens through which we engage with both our digital and physical realities. Without AI, Spatial Computing would not have been possible. It is now with the emergence of Generative AI (Gen AI), that Spatial Computing will be even more augmented.

This juncture is not merely a coming together of technologies; it signifies the opening of a portal to a new era, a threshold to uncharted possibilities. It marries the exceptional data-processing capabilities of AI with the immersive prowess of AR and VR, creating a dynamic synergy. This partnership holds the promise of a transformative future where our interaction with digital information and the world around us is intuitive and seamless, transcending the traditional boundaries between the physical and digital realms.

Intriguingly, the implications of this convergence extend far beyond the realm of technology. It touches various aspects of our daily lives, from how we educate and entertain ourselves to how we receive healthcare and make purchasing decisions. This transformative shift will not only alter the way we interact with technology, but will also redefine the landscape of business.

From a business perspective, the implications are profound. Companies that harness this technology will gain a competitive edge by delivering captivating, immersive experiences to their customers. Consider the medical field, where AR can revolutionize surgeries by providing real-time data to surgeons, or imagine the retail industry, where VR can offer customers the ability to try on clothing virtually. Moreover, the analytical capabilities of AI will facilitate more informed decision-making, a coveted asset in today's dynamic business landscape.

This introduction provides a solid footing for our subsequent exploration of AI and Spatial Computing. Throughout this discussion, we will explore the key components, practical applications, and the far-reaching impact on various sectors. What follows is an in-depth investigation of the convergence that promises to reshape the boundaries between the digital and physical worlds, offering a glimpse into a rapidly evolving present and a promising future that's brimming with opportunities and innovation.

Setting the Stage

In our quest to truly comprehend the significance of this convergence, let's begin by drawing parallels with transformative inventions of the past. History is marked by moments when technological innovations have rewritten the very fabric of human experience. Think back to the groundbreaking invention of the first photograph, which immortalized moments in time and revolutionized the art of visual storytelling. Then came the advent of the first motion picture, which brought narratives to life on the silver screen, ushering in a new era of entertainment and artistic expression.

These pivotal milestones in our history led to tectonic shifts in how we perceive the world. Yet again, we find ourselves at a juncture with AI and Spatial Computing, technologies that stand on the brink of reshaping our lives in profound ways, akin to the revolutionary inventions of the past. Just as the first photograph changed how we document and cherish memories, AI and Spatial Computing are altering our perception of reality. Similar to how motion pictures transformed the entertainment landscape, AR and VR are introducing entirely new dimensions of immersive experiences.

Moreover, just as the introduction of the first television set forever altered the way we connect with the world, AI and Spatial Computing are breaking down the barriers between the physical and digital realms. These technologies enable us to engage with information and environments in previously unimaginable ways.

This convergence isn't merely about the evolution of technology; it signifies a profound shift in how we engage with the world. It has the power to redefine our reality, blurring the lines between the virtual and the physical. It paves the way for a future where our daily lives seamlessly intertwine with AI and Spatial Computing, opening up possibilities beyond our current understanding. As we embark on this exploration of the transformative potential of these technologies, we'll unveil how they are reshaping industries, redefining experiences, and propelling us into an era where innovation and imagination know no bounds.

An AI Moment Unlike Any Other

At this time in history, we find ourselves amid a convergence of two distinctive technological forces, each at a pivotal place in its development. On one hand, there's AI, a technology that has been on an extraordinary evolutionary journey for quite some time. AI's roots can be traced back to the inception of computer science and mathematics, and over the years, it has transformed from abstract concepts into practical applications, becoming an intrinsic part of our daily existence.

Throughout this book, we will explore AI's key components, practical applications, and its far-reaching impact on various sectors. It's imperative to note that Computer Vision (CV) is the driving force behind Spatial Computing. Spatial Computing seamlessly integrates CV, enabling the creation of immersive experiences by understanding and interacting with the physical world. These technologies extend beyond mere vision; they encompass scanning technologies that play a vital role in mapping and interpreting the environment.

Additionally, the influence of GenAI cannot be overstated in the context of Spatial Computing. This technology brings a whole new dimension of 3D creativity, thereby enabling the generation of immersive and interactive 3D content that enriches the Spatial Computing landscape. As we navigate through this book, we will further explore the profound interplay of these technologies and their transformative potential.

The story of AI is marked by significant milestones, from the early days of expert systems, which is software powered by AI that mimics the decision-making expertise of a human specialist in a specific domain to the current era of Machine Learning (ML), Deep Neural Networks, and GAI. Along the way, it has driven innovations like natural language processing, image recognition, and predictive analytics, fundamentally reshaping the way we live and work. The algorithms and models that power AI have grown increasingly sophisticated, empowering intricate decision-making, automation, and personalization across a wide array of industries.

On a parallel route, we encounter Spatial Computing, epitomized by AR and VR, teetering on the precipice of a transition from an evolutionary phase to a revolutionary one. While AR and VR have been evolving for some time, they are now poised to transcend their niche beginnings and achieve more widespread, mainstream adoption. This pivotal moment is significant as it signifies a shift from early enthusiasts to broader and more diverse user bases.

What sets this juncture apart is the profound involvement of AI with Spatial Computing. It's not merely the coexistence of these technologies, but their synergistic potential that holds the power to reshape our world. This convergence is unparalleled, surpassing even transformative events in history, such as the advent of electricity or the impact of the Industrial Revolution. While these past milestones reshaped industries and accelerated progress, the current convergence extends beyond industry and infrastructure to redefine the very essence of human existence.

In addition to its use by CV, AI, with its capability for intricate data analysis, prediction, and decision-making, has already woven itself into the fabric of our lives. It subtly influences our choices, from the content we engage with to the products we select, often working behind the scenes to enhance our experiences. AI has become a silent but ever-present partner in our daily decision-making, consistently striving to enhance efficiency, personalization, and convenience.

In concert, Spatial Computing, with its ability to merge the digital and physical worlds seamlessly, elevates our interactions with technology. It's not just about offering a digital overlay on our physical reality; it's about enabling us to inhabit a context-aware, immersive digital environment. In this spatial dimension, the boundaries between the digital and physical dissolve, unlocking new avenues for interaction and engagement.

This moment signifies a transition from passive consumption of technology to active participation in the digital world. It's a shift from merely observing the digital realm to inhabiting it. The convergence of AI and Spatial Computing promises to redefine not only our daily experiences, but also the very essence of work, education, healthcare, and entertainment.

In essence, this convergence represents a fusion of AI, a technology in ongoing evolution, with the transformative potential of Spatial Computing. It's a bonding that paves the way for a future that is not only technologically advanced, but also profoundly human-centered. It's a moment that holds the promise of unprecedented innovation and transformation, a moment unlike any other in history, where the digital and physical realms unite to create a reality where human potential appears boundless. It's a moment that transcends time and space, defining an era where innovation and imagination combine to redefine the very essence of human interaction and experience.

The Unforgettable Past: 1st Photo, 1st Movie, 1st Television

In the annals of history, let's step back to an era when the very notion of capturing moments in time was revolutionary. The creation of the first photograph was nothing short of a seismic shift in visual representation. It gave humans the profound capability of capturing and immortalizing a profound capability, one to capture and immortalize moments that might otherwise vanish into the mists of history. Through the photograph, we discovered a means to arrest the ephemeral beauty of life, preserving memories in a tangible form for generations to come.

Following this milestone, the emergence of the first motion picture marked an even greater leap in our ability to convey and preserve stories. This technological marvel was a catalyst for narratives, allowing us to experience stories in ways that were once confined to the realm of dreams. The motion picture became the epicenter of entertainment, a medium that bridged gaps and connected people through the universal language of storytelling. It transformed dimly lit theaters into gateways to new worlds, enabling audiences to travel to distant places and bygone eras, all from the comfort of their seats.

And then, the television, another milestone in human history, flickered to life as the first television set was switched on. It was a revelation that introduced the world directly into our living rooms, effectively creating a window to the outside world. Gone were the days when information and entertainment were limited to books and the confines of the radio. The television destroyed the barriers of communication, allowing events from across the globe to unfold visually before our very eyes. News, art, culture, and entertainment were no longer distant; they were now accessible to a wider audience, enriching lives and uniting people across vast distances.

These historic moments from our past serve as poignant reminders of the transformational power of technology. They illuminate how innovation consistently reshapes our world, redefining the ways in which we capture, experience, and communicate the essence of our existence. Similarly, the convergence of AI and Spatial Computing, epitomized by VR and AR, stands as a herald of profound change, poised to reshape how we perceive and interact with our digital and physical realities. This convergence is more than a technological evolution; it represents a paradigm shift, opening a gateway to a future where the boundaries between reality and the virtual realm become more like one. It invites us to participate in an era where innovation and imagination have no bounds, and where our existence intertwines seamlessly, almost magically, within the realm of AI and Spatial Computing.

The Dawn of VR and AR

Today, we stand on the precipice of a technological revolution, reminiscent of earlier paradigm shifts. In this case, it's the emergence of VR and AR that captures our collective imagination. These transformative technologies are redefining how we interact with and perceive the world.

VR, a pioneering innovation, offers the unique capability of transporting individuals into entirely digital environments. When one dons a VR headset, they step into a virtual realm, blurring the boundaries between the physical world and the digital landscape. This immersion enables users to explore synthetic, yet captivatingly lifelike, settings from fantastical realms to lifelike training scenarios. The implications of VR extend far beyond mere entertainment, permeating sectors such as gaming, professional training, and even healthcare, where it replicates real-world situations for educational and skill development purposes.

In contrast, AR follows a different approach. Instead of submerging users in an entirely digital realm, AR superimposes digital elements onto our real-world surroundings. This augmentation enriches our perception and understanding of the physical environment by enhancing it with digital information. AR provides a personalized digital overlay on the real world, offering context and insights that enhance our experiences. Whether it's aiding in city navigation with real-time directions or providing healthcare professionals with crucial patient data during surgical procedures, AR is poised to redefine how we engage with our surroundings.

Both VR and AR transcend the confines of entertainment, making significant inroads into various sectors, including education, healthcare, engineering, and design. In the realm of education, VR provides the opportunity to transport students to historical events or into the inner workings of the human body, transforming learning into an immersive and unforgettable experience. In healthcare, AR empowers surgeons by offering instant access to vital patient data during medical procedures, thereby enhancing surgical precision and patient safety. In architecture and design, both VR and AR facilitate real-time modeling and visualization, enabling professionals to make informed decisions and collaborate more effectively.

The emergence of VR and AR is more than just a technological advancement; it heralds a fundamental shift in the way we learn, work, and enjoy entertainment. These technologies usher in a new era of improved experiential learning, enhanced healthcare practices, and revolutionary contributions to fields such as design and engineering. As we explore the potential of VR and AR, we'll discover how they are shaping the future, creating a reality where the digital and physical realms coexist seamlessly and enhance our lives in myriad ways.

The Promise of Spatial Computing

At the forefront of technology, we find the extraordinary development of Spatial Computing, seamlessly integrating AR and VR. This amalgamation promises to redefine our understanding of human–computer interaction.

The potential of Spatial Computing reaches far beyond mere technological advancement; it envisions a profound revolution in our perception and interaction with the digital and physical realms. In this immersive realm, digital and physical elements meld seamlessly, offering a fundamental shift in how we engage with data, information, and the world around us.

Imagine a future where digital information intricately fuses with your physical environment. In this spatial dimension, digital elements break free from the confines of screens, becoming integral components of your surroundings. Whether you're visualizing intricate data sets in a three-dimensional space, manipulating virtual objects as if they were tangible, or receiving contextually relevant information overlaid onto your physical environment, Spatial Computing not only enhances work, learning, and leisure, but also provides a new lens through which we perceive reality.

The Spatial Computing applications of AR and VR are nothing short of awe-inspiring. They offer the potential to revolutionize a wide array of professions. Architects can seamlessly transition from sketches to immersive, three-dimensional models, allowing them to design and visualize structures in real time. Medical practitioners can utilize AR to provide crucial information during procedures, thereby enhancing precision and safety. In the realm of education, AR and VR offer a new era of experiential learning, allowing students to closely investigate historical events, scientific phenomena, or artistic creations within a spatial context, making education more engaging and unforgettable.

Furthermore, AR and VR have the capacity to redefine collaboration and communication. In this spatial realm, distance becomes irrelevant. Teams can effortlessly collaborate in shared virtual spaces, fostering a sense of togetherness regardless of physical distances. This collaborative potential extends across various fields, including design, where professionals can work together on projects in real time, irrespective of their physical locations. In the field of healthcare, AR and VR enable telemedicine to reach new heights as medical experts can guide procedures through AR overlays, transcending geographical boundaries.

The promise of AR and VR extends far beyond the boundaries of technology; it redefines our reality and unleashes boundless potential. As we stand on the threshold of this transformative era, we enter a world where the lines between the digital and physical realms dissolve, paving the way for a tapestry of opportunities. Innovation knows no bounds in this landscape, where AR and VR enhance every facet of our lives, promising a future where the realms of the real and the virtual seamlessly merge to create a richer, more immersive existence.

The Imperative for Leaders

In the dynamically shifting domain of technology, established leaders—and those aspiring to take the helm—are confronted not with a mere choice, but with a serious obligation to immerse themselves in the profound insights provided in this book. In an era where the pace of technological convergence is nothing short of breathtaking, the ability to remain skilled, informed, and competitive in this ever-shifting terrain has transcended the realm of importance to become a paramount necessity.

At the heart of this imperative lies a fundamental truth that resonates with crystalline clarity in the world of technology: "AI won't replace your job, but someone working with AI will." This succinct statement encapsulates the crux of our current reality. It recognizes the irreplaceable role of human expertise, while underscoring the symbiotic relationship between human intellect and the capabilities of AI. It's not a matter of humans versus machines; rather, it's about humans collaborating with AI to unlock unprecedented potential.

In the chapters that follow, we will embark on an extensive exploration of the multifaceted landscape of AI and Spatial Computing. This journey will take us through a comprehensive understanding of their significance, their far-reaching applications spanning across various domains, and the multifaceted skill set required to adeptly navigate this perpetually shifting terrain.

The integration of these frontiers, AI and Spatial Computing, is not merely a confluence of technologies; it represents a burst of possibilities and opportunities. These are not passing trends but transformative forces, reshaping industries, redefining business models, and revolutionizing the way we interact with technology and the world at large.

Leaders bear a significant responsibility in this evolving landscape. It is incumbent on them not only to comprehend the intricacies of AI and Spatial Computing, but also to lead the charge in harnessing their capabilities effectively. Embracing these frontiers is the key to remaining at the vanguard of innovation. It's about steering organizations into a future where adaptability, innovation, and technological fluency are the cornerstones of success.

As a leader, your role extends beyond steering the ship; it's about having the vision and the courage to set sail in uncharted waters. It's about guiding your teams with confidence, knowing that the convergence of AI and Spatial Computing is a journey that promises not just technological advancement, but profound human-centered transformation. It's about shaping an organizational culture that is not only prepared for the future, but also poised to thrive in it.

The future beckons with tantalizing prospects and exciting possibilities. In this era, leadership is not just about managing change; it's about embracing it, leading with a sense of curiosity and courage, and seizing the transformative power of these converging frontiers. The leaders of tomorrow are those who understand that innovation is boundless, and that by embracing change and harnessing the capabilities of AI and Spatial Computing, we can create a future that's not only technologically advanced, but also deeply human-centric. Let's embark on this journey of exploration and transformation with determination and foresight. The future beckons, and we must be prepared to embrace it.

In our next section, we reveal the essence of Spatial Computing within the business context, and begin by exploring its fundamental definition and the core technologies it entails.

What Is *Spatial Computing*?

Spatial Computing is a term that many in the business world might have heard for the first time during Apple's announcement of their Apple Vision Pro device in June 2023. But, it is by no means a new term. One could argue that our mobile phones are primitive spatial devices. The reality is that many professionals in AR, VR, XR, and AI have been working on Spatial Computing for years.

To appreciate the business value of Spatial Computing, we first have to create a working definition for the business world and explain the market opportunities it will enable.

Once we do that, we can understand how business and computing will change in order to prepare for this transformation.

Many trace the first time Spatial Computing was defined as an academic term to Simon Greenwold's 2003 MIT master thesis when he was a researcher in the Aesthetics and Computation group at the MIT Media Lab. In his thesis, he explores spatial contexts for computational constructs and defines *Spatial Computing* as: "Spatial computing is human interaction with a machine in which the machine retains and manipulates referents to real objects and spaces. It is an essential component for making our machines fuller partners in our work and play."

He went on to define it further, "as human interaction with a machine in which the machine retains and manipulates referents to real objects and spaces. Ideally, these real objects and spaces have prior significance to the user. Spatial computing is more interested in qualities of experience. Mostly, it means designing systems that push through the traditional boundaries of screen and keyboard without getting hung up there and melting into an interface or meek simulation. In order for our machines to become fuller partners in our work and play, they are going to need to join us in our physical world. They are going to have to operate on the same objects we do, and we are going to need to operate on them using our physical intuitions."

Greenwold's definition isn't the only one out there. Very early on, Magic Leap, once one of the darlings of the venture capital and tech world, described the device they were building as a Spatial Computing device. They defined *Spatial Computing* as a new form of computing that uses AI and CV to seamlessly blend virtual content into the physical world around us.

They did this through a device called the Magic Leap One. In a 2018 article entitled "Spatial Computing: An Overview for our Techie Friends," written by former CEO Rony Abovitz and several other prominent Magic Leap employees, they explained how the company defined Spatial Computing as a new form of computing that allows digital content to move beyond the confines of the 2D screens and computers of today and dive deeper into some of its technical components.[1] Since then, Magic Leap has pivoted away from using the term Spatial Computing to using the term *AR*, as seen in its most recent media interviews and on its website.

During Apple's June 2023 Worldwide Developers Conference (WWDC), the company publicly stated that Spatial Computing, "seamlessly blends digital content with the physical world while allowing users to stay present and connected to others." This messaging is further reflected on its website and its literature for visionOS for developers.

During the Meta Connect 2023 developer's conference, Meta announced the launch of its Meta Quest 3, which uses new chips that allow the device to deliver good pass-through mixed reality, better scanning of the physical world through advanced spatial mapping, and spatial anchoring of virtual objects that wearers can come back to each time they use the device. Meta executives also spoke about ushering the next computing platform through advancements in smart glasses and stated that the company's new headset will be the "best value Spatial Computing headset on the market for a long time to come."

The company also announced its new Ray-Ban Meta Smart Glasses, which became multimodal in 2024, allowing the glasses to understand the environment around wearers using AI. Microsoft has defined this as the ability of devices to be aware of their surroundings and to represent the awareness digitally and to offer novel capabilities in human-robot interaction.

While Amazon Web Services (AWS) defines Spatial Computing as the combination of the virtual and physical worlds that allows users to interact with digital content in a natural and intuitive way, by allowing our physical world to be virtualized and by overlaying virtual information onto the physical world. To AWS, this combination enhances how we visualize, simulate, and interact with data in physical or virtual locations. In his post, "The Best Way to Predict the Future Is to Simulate It," Amazon VP of Technology Bill Vass stated, "Spatial Computing is what powers collaborative experiences."[2]

While Nvidia has introduced spatial frameworks for its developers through its Omniverse efforts, Niantic has focused on spatial mapping through its Visual Positioning System (VPS), which enables users to place virtual objects in a specific real-world location and have that object persist, so one person can leave an object for someone else to find, bringing real-world global game boards to life.

Defining Spatial Computing for Today's Business World

A working definition of Spatial Computing is needed so we are all in tandem with this new technology. A solid definition will help to make sense of Spatial Computing throughout the business world and how it will impact the future of business, work, education, shopping, leisure, and more.

Spatial computing is the next shift in how humans interact with technology. It involves a range of technologies, from AI, Extended Reality (XR), Internet of Things (IoT), sensors, and more, in order to empower and create a new form of human and computer interaction—one that is more immersive and impactful than ever before. Spatial Computing will reinvent human–computer interaction that is currently inherently spatial. In other words, it will allow for a three-dimensionality that lends itself to more realistic representations and interactions.

Spatial Computing uses information about the environment to act in a way that's most intuitive for the person using it. How businesses digitally transform using Spatial Computing will set them apart from the competition, and set them up for success for the next generation that grew up in an increasingly blended virtual and physical world.

Spatial Computing will bring with it utility and impactful use cases. It will allow workers to easily bring their workstations with them—a form of screen replacement—an infinite canvas. Through AI, Spatial Computing will usher in a new way of communicating with computers and machines, where those machines are able to interpret our world and enable a new paradigm of human–computer interaction.

Today's rudimentary AR that we experience on our phones is planting the seeds for tomorrow's Spatial Computing. We are already seeing the early signs of Spatial Computing user interfaces (UIs). Spatial Computing will remove barriers, shorten distances, and enable large-scale collaboration at levels humanity has never experienced before. It will materialize the internet and its data in our physical space via a spatial computer. Through the use of technologies, the spatial computer will understand the wearer and their physical space, which in turn, becomes updatable and interactive in real time. It comes "alive." It allows for more intuitive and natural interactions with our computers and enables our devices to better understand, map, and navigate our physical environment. These devices will see what we see and learn about our world. In some ways, it allows us to interact with the virtual world with the same ease we do with the physical world.

Humans are naturally spatial beings who understand and engage with the world volumetrically, so Spatial Computing promises to return us to spatial thinking that is very often lost as we age and when we are forced to translate our creativity into flat surfaces. Its promise is to make us more productive, efficient, creative, and to facilitate communication with others. Spatial Computing can eventually lead to making better decisions, whether in business or in other aspects of our lives. It's an evolutionary technological shift away from static devices that must hang on our walls, sit on our desks, or rest in our hands to devices that start to fade into the background and allow us to go back to focusing on the physical space around us, albeit augmented.

While we are living at this moment through an AI revolution, we are at the cusp of a new computing paradigm where what's physical and what's virtual converge seamlessly, opening up endless possibilities for creativity, innovation, human connectivity, and new ways to work. This has profound implications for how we interact with technology and with each other. It removes barriers, closes distances, and enables co-presence. Spatial Computing will force us to explore the convergence between the physical and the virtual. In other words, it will make the devices we use and how we use them blend into the daily natural flow and patterns of how we live our lives.

Spatial Computing brings digital information and experiences into a physical environment. It takes into account the position, orientation, and context of the wearer as well as the objects and surfaces around it. It uses a new, advanced type of computing to understand the physical world in relation to virtual environments and the wearer. It does this by using emerging interfaces like wearable headsets that have cameras, scanners, microphones, and other sensors built into the device. New interfaces come in the form of hand gestures and finger movements, gaze tracking, and voice. Global Positioning system (GPS), Bluetooth, and other sensors make creating digital content with physical context possible.

From shopping to working and from planning to playing, the world around us will engage with us in new ways via Spatial Computing. It's where computing, communication, and 3D converge. Spatial computing enables advanced gestural recognition (like recognizing our hand motions and applying them as commands), and it will have better-than-4K resolution images for each eye.

So, how does this differ from VR and AR? Spatial Computing may not seem different from Virtual Reality or Augmented Reality. AR is overlaying digital content into a physical space. VR is a completely immersive virtual environment. The XR spectrum is part of Spatial Computing, but it's not its only enabling technology. AI is on everyone's mind, along with XR, sensors, IoT, and new levels of connectivity. AI is one of the most important underlying technologies that will bring Spatial Computing to the masses.

In other words, Spatial Computing is a mix of hardware and software that enables machines to understand our physical environment without us telling so, and in turn, it enables us to create content, products, and services that have purpose in both physical and virtual environments. Spatial Computing is a transformative new way of engaging with technology that seamlessly blends the physical and virtual worlds through the use of a range of technologies and allows us to navigate the world alongside robots, drones, cars, virtual assistants, and beyond.

The future of Spatial Computing is poised for substantial growth, driven by key advancements. These include radical progress in optics, the miniaturization of sensors and chips, the ability to authentically portray 3D images, and the continuous evolution of Spatial Computing hardware and software. These innovations, supported by significant breakthroughs in AI, will make Spatial Computing increasingly compelling for businesses on a grand scale in the years to come.

Here's the working definition that we present for business professionals to use. This definition is a polished version of what was first used in an article Cathy wrote for the *Harvard Business Review* in November 2023 that the authors worked on to refine.

> Spatial Computing is an evolving 3D-centric form of computing that, at its core, uses AI, Computer Vision, and Extended Reality to blend virtual experiences into the physical world that break free from screens and make all surfaces spatial interfaces. It allows humans, devices, computers, robots, and virtual beings to navigate through computing in 3D space. It ushers in a new paradigm for human-to-human interaction as well as human–computer interaction, enhancing how we visualize, simulate, and interact with data in physical or virtual locations and expanding computing beyond the confines of the screen into everything you can see, experience, and know.
>
> Spatial Computing allows us to navigate the world alongside robots, drones, cars, virtual assistants, and beyond, but it is not limited to just one technology or just one device. It is a mix of software, hardware, and information that allows humans and technology to connect in new ways ushering in a new form of computing that could be even more impactful than personal computing and mobile computing have been to society.

In an effort to provide clarity, we must also discuss what Spatial Computing isn't. It is not just XR, and it is not just one device or one single company. It is a sea-change in how humans engage with technology.

When we are asked about the difference between Spatial Computing and a concept like the Metaverse (which Cathy and Irena have written about and worked extensively in), this tweet (X post) from Andrew Schwartz, Director of Metaverse Engineering at Nike, points out why Spatial Computing could be transformative and how it differs from the Metaverse. "If the organizing principle of the internet is that information wants to be shared, and the organizing principle of the metaverse is that information wants to be experienced, Spatial Computing brings together the tools necessary to create those experiences," he wrote.

Spatial Computing is an enabler of new tech shifts, but it is also enabled by a range of technologies that we will dive into deeper in the next section and throughout the book.

What Are the Technologies?

The world of Spatial Computing relies on a set of essential technologies that drive its immersive experiences. These technologies range from AI and content-creation tools to connectivity solutions and cloud computing. In this section, we'll explore each of these technologies and their pivotal roles in the realm of Spatial Computing, where the digital and physical worlds merge to create extraordinary experiences.

The AI Foundation

AI serves as the bedrock of Spatial Computing, incorporating various subfields:

Machine Learning (ML): ML is the backbone of Spatial Computing, enabling systems to learn from data and adapt without being explicitly programmed. It allows machines to recognize patterns, make decisions, and improve their performance over time. In Spatial Computing, ML powers applications like route planning in AR navigation, where real-time sensor data is analyzed to offer users the most efficient and user-friendly routes. ML plays a critical role in enhancing user experiences by constantly refining its understanding of the environment.

Deep Learning (DL): DL is a subset of ML that focuses on the use of neural networks with multiple layers to model complex patterns. In Spatial Computing, DL enables the creation of intricate models that can process vast amounts of data, making it essential for image recognition and object detection in AR and VR applications. This technology enhances the ability of spatial devices to identify and interact with objects and spaces within the user's surroundings.

Reinforcement Learning (RL): RL is a form of ML where an agent learns to make decisions by taking actions and receiving feedback or rewards. In Spatial Computing, RL is employed to develop dynamic character behavior in gaming and entertainment applications. It allows characters to adapt their actions based on user input, creating more immersive and interactive experiences. Furthermore, RL contributes to the real-time decision-making processes used in spatial devices to improve user interaction.

Procedural Generation: Procedural Generation is a technique used to generate content algorithmically, creating vast and varied landscapes, objects, and scenarios. In Spatial Computing, Procedural Generation brings a dynamic and ever-changing dimension to immersive environments. This technology is often used to generate 3D worlds, making each user's experience unique. It is crucial for applications, such as gaming, virtual simulations, and AR, where content needs to be generated on the fly to maintain freshness and variety.

Neural Networks: Neural Networks are computational models inspired by the human brain's structure. They are fundamental for various AI tasks, including pattern recognition and data analysis. In Spatial Computing, Neural Networks contribute to complex processing tasks. For instance, they play a pivotal role in CV, enabling the recognition of objects and shapes in the real world. This capability is central to the augmentation of the physical environment in AR applications, providing real-time information and enhancing user understanding.

Computer Vision (CV): CV is the technology that empowers machines to understand and interpret visual information from the physical world. In Spatial Computing, CV is at the forefront, allowing spatial devices to identify and interact with objects and spaces within a user's surroundings. It is instrumental in applications like AR navigation, which overlays digital information onto the real world, providing users with real-time directions and guidance.

Sensor technology: Sensor technology is the sensory nervous system of Spatial Computing, providing devices with the capability to perceive the physical world. Spatial devices are equipped with a variety of sensors, including cameras, gyroscopes, accelerometers, GPS, Light Detection and Ranging (LiDAR), and more. These sensors capture data about the user's surroundings, such as motion, location, light levels, and even depth information. In Spatial Computing, sensors play a pivotal role in understanding the user's environment and movements, facilitating precise tracking, gesture recognition, and the mapping of physical spaces. These sensors are the eyes and ears of spatial devices, enabling them to provide real-time, context-aware experiences to users. Whether it's for immersive gaming, AR navigation, or precise mapping of industrial environments, sensor technology is essential for creating dynamic and interactive spatial experiences.

Spatial audio: Spatial audio is the unsung hero of immersive experiences in the realm of Spatial Computing. It transforms the way we perceive sound, immersing us in a three-dimensional auditory landscape that aligns with the visual aspects of the environment. Whether you're exploring a virtual world, attending a virtual concert, or engaging in AR storytelling, spatial audio adds depth, dimension, and realism to the auditory component of the experience. It allows sounds to originate from specific points in space, creating a sense of direction and distance, and even simulating the acoustics of different environments. Spatial audio not only enriches our entertainment and gaming experiences, but also finds applications in training simulations, virtual meetings, and architectural design. This technology revolutionizes the way we engage with sound, making audio an integral part of the immersive journey.

Eye tracking: Eye-tracking technology has emerged as a game-changer in Spatial Computing, offering a direct window into users' intentions and interests. By precisely monitoring eye movements and gaze direction, it enables more natural and intuitive interactions with spatial devices. From

VR and AR to gaming and healthcare applications, eye tracking enhances user experiences. It allows devices to adapt based on where users are looking, offering targeted information, improved immersion, and even personalizing content. Beyond entertainment, eye tracking holds significant promise in healthcare, assisting individuals with mobility impairments, and aiding in diagnostic procedures. With this technology, the act of looking becomes a powerful tool for navigating and shaping the digital and physical world in ways that were previously unimaginable.

Voice recognition: Voice recognition technology has become the cornerstone of effortless communication in the world of Spatial Computing, elevated by the capabilities of AI. With the power of speech, users can interact with spatial devices naturally, issuing commands, asking questions, and receiving responses with just their voices. AI algorithms underpin voice recognition, allowing these systems to understand the nuances of human language, accents, and context. This technology not only brings convenience to daily tasks, but also opens doors to accessibility, allowing individuals of all abilities to engage with spatial environments. Whether it's navigating AR interfaces, controlling smart-home devices, or having real-time language translation at your fingertips, voice recognition, enhanced by AI, has become the bridge that connects human intent to digital action. In the rapidly evolving landscape of Spatial Computing, voice recognition is the symphony that harmonizes our words with the actions and experiences we desire.

Anomaly Detection: Anomaly Detection involves identifying unusual patterns or behaviors in data. In Spatial Computing, this technology is crucial for ensuring safety and security. By analyzing sensor data and identifying anomalies, spatial devices can alert users to potential issues. Anomaly Detection is particularly vital in applications related to predictive maintenance, where it helps predict equipment failures and reduces downtime.

Physics-Based Simulation: Physics-Based Simulation is essential for creating realistic and dynamic virtual environments in Spatial Computing. It allows spatial applications to mimic real-world physical interactions, enhancing the user's sense of presence and interaction. Medical training simulations, architectural design, and gaming applications leverage this technology to provide realistic scenarios and user experiences.

Optimization Algorithms: Optimization Algorithms are fundamental for streamlining processes and decision-making in Spatial Computing. They ensure that systems operate efficiently and effectively. In applications like retail store layout optimization, these algorithms analyze customer movement data and help retailers enhance the shopping experience by optimizing store layouts and product placements.

Natural Language Processing (NLP): NLP enables machines to understand and interact with human language. In Spatial Computing, NLP facilitates seamless communication between users and spatial devices. It is particularly crucial for applications involving real-time language translation, where AR glasses can provide instant translation of spoken language into subtitles or audio, allowing individuals who speak different languages to communicate effortlessly.

Speech recognition: Speech recognition is the technology that converts spoken language into textual or actionable data. In Spatial Computing, this technology is instrumental for user interaction. It enables users to issue voice commands and receive responses from spatial devices, making voice-controlled interfaces an integral part of AR and VR applications.

Generative AI (GenAI): GenAI is a technology that brings a new dimension of creativity to Spatial Computing. It empowers applications to create 3D content and simulations, expanding the possibilities for immersive experiences. For instance, in the realm of fashion design and luxury, GenAI is used to process volumetric data, analyze supply chain information, and generate virtual 3D models of products and designs.

These technologies collectively form the AI framework of Spatial Computing, infusing it with the capabilities to interact, adapt, and innovate within the real world.

Other Key Technologies Tied to Spatial Computing

In the multifaceted world of Spatial Computing, several key technologies collaboratively underpin the creation of immersive experiences. These technologies encompass content creation and design tools, rendering and graphics, cloud and edge computing, high-speed connectivity, and integration with the IoT. Each of these components plays a distinct and vital role in shaping the landscape of Spatial Computing, enhancing everything from visuals to computational capabilities and broader connectivity. Let's delve into the significance of these technologies and how they empower the Spatial Computing ecosystem.

Content creation and design tools: Content creation and design tools are the artisans behind the immersive experiences of Spatial Computing. They empower creators to build interactive and captivating spatial content, whether it's virtual worlds, AR apps, or 3D models. These tools facilitate the design of spatial environments, objects, and characters, allowing for the seamless integration of digital elements into the physical world. Content creation and design tools are the brushes and canvases of the spatial artist, enabling the translation of imaginative concepts into tangible, experiential realities.

Rendering and graphics: Rendering and graphics are the canvas on which the realistic visual experiences of Spatial Computing come to life. Whether you're exploring a virtual landscape or interacting with Augmented Reality overlays, the quality of the visual experience depends on the prowess of rendering and graphics technologies. These systems handle the intricate process of translating digital information into visually stunning representations. They encompass everything from lighting and shadows to texture and color, ensuring that what you see in the spatial realm is not just convincing but awe-inspiring.

Cloud and Edge Computing: Cloud and Edge Computing serve as the dynamic duo that powers the computational and storage needs of Spatial Computing. The cloud provides the vast reservoir of data and processing capabilities required for sophisticated spatial experiences. It enables seamless data synchronization and access across multiple devices. On the other hand, Edge Computing brings real-time processing closer to the spatial devices, reducing latency and ensuring that interactions happen instantaneously. Together, they create the backbone of Spatial Computing, offering the computational muscle and storage capacity to realize its full potential.

5G/6G connectivity: 5G and the emerging 6G connectivity are the superhighways of Spatial Computing, ensuring fast and reliable data transfer between devices and the cloud. These technologies underpin the seamless exchange of information in real-time, enabling high-quality, low-latency spatial experiences. Whether it's streaming AR content, collaborating on a virtual project, or gaming in a shared virtual space, 5G and 6G connectivity are the vital infrastructure that ensures smooth and uninterrupted connections.

IoT integration: IoT integration is the connecting thread that bridges spatial devices with the broader world of interconnected devices and systems. In Spatial Computing, it's not just about the interaction between devices; it's about how these devices fit into the larger ecosystem of interconnected technologies. IoT integration allows spatial devices to communicate with smart-home appliances, city infrastructure, healthcare systems, and more. It expands the possibilities of what Spatial Computing can achieve by creating a network of devices that work together to enhance our daily lives and experiences.

Real-World Use Case Examples

Exploring a spectrum of compelling AI-driven applications in Spatial Computing—from reimagining navigation to predictive maintenance, these real-world examples highlight the dynamic role AI plays in shaping transformative experiences within the spatial realm:

AR navigation: AI algorithms in AR navigation apps revolutionize the way we navigate our surroundings. These apps provide real-time directions and location-based information, overlaying intuitive visual cues, such as arrows and street names, onto users' views. Whether it's finding the quickest route through a bustling city or discovering hidden gems in an unfamiliar place, AI-enhanced navigation simplifies the journey.

Virtual interior design: Spatial Computing, coupled with AI, transforms the way we envision interior design. AI-powered apps enable users to visualize furniture and decor within their homes. By employing CV to identify room layouts and design preferences, these apps offer tailored design suggestions. It's a game-changer for homeowners and interior designers, providing a realistic preview of design choices before any physical changes are made.

Predictive maintenance in industrial settings: The marriage of AI and Spatial Computing in industrial settings results in predictive maintenance solutions. AI algorithms analyze sensor data from machines and equipment, forecasting potential failures before they occur. By reducing downtime and improving operational efficiency, this application saves businesses time and resources, which ultimately enhances productivity.

Medical training simulations: Healthcare professionals are embracing AI-driven simulations within VR environments. These simulations offer a risk-free space for medical practitioners to practice surgeries and procedures. AI augments these scenarios by providing realistic feedback, enabling healthcare providers to refine their surgical skills, ultimately enhancing patient safety, recovery, and post-surgical care.

Retail store layout optimization: AI finds a profound application in retail, optimizing store layouts and product placements. By analyzing customer movement patterns using Spatial Computing, retailers can create shopping experiences that are both engaging and profitable. AI helps businesses enhance the flow of shoppers and align product placements with customer behavior.

Fashion design and luxury: Fashion and luxury industries leverage AI to optimize supply chains, track evolving fashion trends, and revolutionize design. AI in fashion integrates CV to process volumetric data for accurate fit and precision. Machine learning helps analyze supply chain data and enhance processes, while GenAI introduces 3D virtual models, thus changing the landscape of fashion design.

Smart city planning: AI is a driving force behind informed urban planning, where it analyzes data from sensors and cameras throughout a city. Spatial computing assists in visualizing this data, helping city planners make informed decisions about traffic management, infrastructure development, and public safety. AI ensures cities are optimized for efficient and sustainable growth.

Real-time language translation: The synergy of AI and Spatial Computing facilitates real-time language translation. AR glasses, powered by AI, convert spoken language into subtitles or audio, enabling seamless communication between individuals who speak different languages. This technology transcends language barriers, fostering collaboration and understanding in a globalized world.

Safety audits and inspections: AI-powered AR glasses revolutionize safety audits and inspections in industrial settings. These smart glasses identify potential hazards and compliance issues in real time. They enhance workplace safety by providing safety auditors with valuable information to prevent accidents and ensure regulatory compliance.

Architectural design and visualization: Architects are embracing AI and Spatial Computing to create 3D virtual models of buildings and urban environments. These models enable architects to visualize and iterate on designs more effectively, enhancing precision and creativity in the architectural field.

Gaming and entertainment: AI-driven algorithms enhance the gaming and entertainment experiences in VR and AR. Reinforcement Learning is applied to character behavior, providing dynamic and adaptive gameplay. Procedural Generation techniques generate realistic 3D environments, while Neural Networks contribute to character behavior and environmental generation, making gaming and entertainment experiences more immersive and interactive.

In this section, we've uncovered the pivotal technologies driving Spatial Computing's immersive experiences, from AI and its subfields to other key technological components. These technologies collectively shape the landscape where the physical and digital worlds merge to create extraordinary experiences. Now, let's shift our focus to the benefactors who harness the power of these technologies.

Who Are the Beneficiaries?

Spatial Computing has brought forth a wave of transformative benefits, reaching a broad spectrum of beneficiaries across various sectors and walks of life that could then potentially become benefactors for those in Spatial Computing. This technology has fundamentally altered the way we interact with the digital and physical worlds, offering a host of advantages. Let's explore who these beneficiaries are and how they are harnessing the potential of Spatial Computing for their specific needs and objectives.

Major Beneficiaries

Consumers and end users: The most significant beneficiaries of Spatial Computing are consumers and end users. They experience immersive entertainment, from AR games to VR simulations, providing a new dimension of enjoyment and engagement. Additionally, in education and training, end users benefit from realistic and interactive learning experiences, shaping the future of knowledge transfer.

Healthcare: Spatial Computing plays a pivotal role in the healthcare sector. Medical professionals employ this technology for surgical planning and training, offering surgeons a risk-free environment to practice complex procedures. Patients, on the other hand, gain from advanced visualization and telemedicine applications, receiving improved diagnostics and treatment options.

Manufacturing and industrial: Manufacturers have found a valuable ally in Spatial Computing. It aids in product design, prototyping, and quality control, reducing time-to-market and enhancing product quality. Maintenance and repair technicians also reap the benefits, accessing AR instructions that enhance efficiency and reduce errors.

Retail: Retailers have harnessed Spatial Computing to elevate the shopping experience. AR shopping allows customers to visualize products in their own space before making a purchase decision, reducing the uncertainty of online shopping. Additionally, inventory management and logistics benefit from improved spatial understanding and automation.

Fashion and luxury: The Fashion and luxury industries are experiencing a transformation through Spatial Computing. It accelerates design, fit, and personalization of garments, both ready-to-wear and made-to-order. Spatial computing devices themselves become fashion statements, while gaming and entertainment blend with fashion to open new revenue streams.

Gaming and entertainment: The gaming industry is at the forefront of Spatial Computing, offering gamers immersive and interactive experiences through VR and AR. Meanwhile, the entertainment sector crafts captivating VR and AR experiences, enhancing performances and events with AR overlays.

Education and training: Educational institutions leverage Spatial Computing for interactive and engaging lessons, making complex subjects more accessible. Training in various fields, such as aviation and military, benefits from realistic simulations that enhance learning.

Real estate and architecture: Real estate professionals employ Spatial Computing for showcasing properties with virtual tours and AR visualizations, streamlining the buying and selling process. Architects and urban planners benefit from 3D modeling for precise design and client presentations.

Transportation and automotive: Spatial Computing advances autonomous vehicle development, improving navigation and safety systems. Public transportation benefits from improved route planning and passenger information, enhancing the travel experience.

Aerospace and defense: The aerospace industry relies on Spatial Computing for aircraft design, maintenance, and pilot training. Defense applications encompass advanced simulations and training scenarios for military personnel.

Art and creativity: Artists and designers embrace Spatial Computing tools for digital art creation and 3D modeling. It introduces new forms of interactive and immersive art installations that redefine the boundaries of creativity.

Construction: In the construction industry, Spatial Computing aids workers in visualizing architectural plans, detecting errors before construction commences.

Tourism and cultural heritage: Tourists benefit from AR-guided tours and interactive cultural experiences at museums and historical sites. Cultural heritage preservation relies on 3D scanning and digital archiving to protect and celebrate our past.

Environmental science: Spatial Computing finds applications in environmental science, assisting researchers in environmental monitoring and data visualization, contributing to conservation efforts and a sustainable future.

Accessibility: Spatial Computing fosters accessibility through adaptive interfaces and assistive technologies, ensuring individuals with disabilities can engage with digital content and environments.

Enterprise and productivity: Businesses harness the power of Spatial Computing for enhanced collaboration, remote work, and data visualization. It elevates decision-making processes and data analysis, offering a competitive edge in the modern business landscape.

These beneficiaries represent a diverse and dynamic landscape that thrives on the capabilities and innovations brought about by Spatial Computing, shaping industries, improving lives, and pushing the boundaries of what's possible.

Why Good for Business?

Spatial Computing and AI are changing the business world as we know it. They are already bringing value to businesses through a myriad of use cases. AI is at the forefront of showing the value that technology can bring, while Spatial Computing is more of a dormant giant waiting to be awakened in the next decade.

So what is the business value of Spatial Computing and AI? Following is a short non-exhaustive list of some of the benefits we have identified and which we will be analyzing in a deeper way and expanding on in the chapters to come.

Spatial computing and AI are good for business because they can:

- Optimize and improve processes.
- Facilitate communication and collaboration in new innovative ways.
- Solve communication problems.
- Offer better retail experiences, which can lead to fewer returns and a reduction in waste.
- Create more immersive entertainment that can delight customers.
- Create new ways of preserving memories and history through the use of spatial video and memory capture. (We believe this will be one of the main reasons consumers will buy a spatial computer.)
- Help combat climate change through better modeling and better tools, as well as make better decisions.
- Have impactful potential for diplomacy and better decision-making, as well as visualization for strategic foresight,
- And more!

We wholeheartedly believe that the convergence of Spatial Computing and AI will change business as we know it and will have a visible impact on your life. We wrote this book to help you navigate this new reality. We also wrote it to help today's and tomorrow's leaders be better prepared to lead and make strategic use of these technologies, not as a fad but as part of the future of business.

This is what you should expect from reading our book. In this Introduction, we set the stage for why AI and Spatial Computing are crucial for the modern business leader.

In the next three chapters (Chapters 1, 2, and 3), we will focus on the business relevance of AI-driven Spatial Computing. In Chapters 4, 5, and 6, we will cover what leaders need to know about the convergence of Spatial Computing and AI in this new era and how they can successfully lead their organizations during this time of rapid technological change.

In the final three chapters of the book (Chapters 7, 8, and 9), we will focus on the strategy needed to succeed, as well as how to implement Spatial Computing and AI. We will then venture into what the future of this AI-driven business revolution could bring!

So, in the chapters to come, we will dive deep into how AI and Spatial Computing are changing business, who the leaders that are already having an impact are, and why understanding Spatial Computing and AI at this juncture is critical to lead the businesses of today into the future. So get ready to expand your thinking beyond just AI and start to look at the bigger picture. The future is about the convergence of both AI and Spatial Computing!

SPATIAL
COMPUTING

PART 1

The Business Relevance of AI-Driven Spatial Computing

CHAPTER 1

The AI Revolution: Transforming Today's Business

From Aristotle to Today

AI has undergone a remarkable transformation from a mere concept in the annals of science fiction to a pivotal force in contemporary technology and industry. This evolution is a testament to human ingenuity and a reflection of our enduring quest to create intelligent machines.

The conception and evolution of AI have been significantly influenced by philosophical thought, stretching back centuries before the advent of contemporary technology. The inquiries and speculations of ancient, medieval, and early modern philosophers laid a conceptual groundwork that subtly prefigured the development of AI.

In ancient and medieval times, myths and storytelling often featured elements of artificial life and mechanical beings. For example, ancient Greek myths recounted tales of Hephaestus, the god of blacksmiths, who created mechanical servants. These stories reflect an early human fascination with the idea of artificial beings and the possibility of mimicking life or human intelligence.

The contributions of Aristotle, the ancient Greek philosopher, were foundational, particularly in the realm of logic. His work on syllogisms, a form of logical reasoning, and his ideas about categorizing knowledge and deductive reasoning can be seen as early steps toward algorithmic thinking, a cornerstone of modern AI.

During the Renaissance, there was a surge of interest in automata—mechanical devices designed to imitate human or animal actions. These devices, often powered by intricate clockwork mechanisms, were the precursors to modern robotics. The Renaissance marked a period where the intersection of art, science, and technology began to blur, setting a precedent for today's AI innovations.

René Descartes, an Enlightenment philosopher, proposed the concept of mind-body dualism, which separated the mind from the physical world. While his views were more metaphysical than technological, they initiated discussions about the nature of consciousness and intelligence. These debates are central to the philosophical underpinnings of AI, especially when considering the possibility of machine consciousness or sentience.

In the 19th century, figures like Charles Babbage and Ada Lovelace, though not philosophers in the traditional sense, made significant contributions that bridged philosophy and early computing. Babbage's design of the Analytical Engine and Lovelace's recognition of its potential to go beyond mere calculation laid foundational ideas for computational machines and AI.

George Boole, a mathematician and logician of the same era, developed a system of logical algebra that formed the basis for digital circuit design and computer programming. Boolean algebra, with its binary variables, became a critical element in the development of computing and AI.

The early 20th century saw the rise of logical positivism and the Vienna Circle, a group of philosophers and scientists advocating a scientific approach to philosophy grounded in logic and empirical data. This movement influenced later thinking in AI, particularly in the development of algorithms that mimic human reasoning.

Alan Turing, known for his contributions to computer science, also engaged with philosophical questions about machine intelligence. His Turing Test, while a technical proposition, was equally a philosophical one, prompting considerations about when a machine might be regarded as truly "intelligent."

Despite these promising beginnings, AI's journey was not without its challenges. The field experienced periods of high optimism, followed by disappointment and reduced funding, known as "AI winters." These winters were largely due to the limitations of technology at the time, which could not keep pace with the theoretical aspirations of AI researchers.

However, the resurgence of AI in the late 20th and early 21st centuries was fueled by significant advancements in computational power and the availability of large datasets. These developments enabled the creation of more sophisticated ML models and Neural Networks, which could learn and improve from vast amounts of data. DL, a subset of ML involving layered Neural Networks, became a driving force behind many of AI's most impressive feats, from mastering complex games to driving advancements in NLP and image recognition.

The impact of AI has been profound and far-reaching, infiltrating a multitude of industries and aspects of daily life. In manufacturing, AI-driven automation and predictive maintenance have revolutionized production lines. In finance, AI algorithms are used for tasks ranging from fraud detection to algorithmic trading. The healthcare sector has seen significant benefits from AI in areas like diagnostic imaging, drug discovery, and personalized medicine.

AI's influence extends beyond industry to touch the lives of individuals through consumer technologies. Smart assistants, personalized recommendations on streaming platforms, and sophisticated algorithms that moderate content on social media are all examples of AI in action. And more to the point, AI has enhanced the capabilities of Spatial Computing technologies, making them more interactive and immersive.

AI, serving as a foundational component of Spatial Computing, enables the integration of digital and physical spaces in ways that were once the domain of science fiction. To understand the full scope of AI's role in Spatial Computing, it's essential to explore the evolution of AI technologies and applications, the various categories of AI software, and specific fields like NLP, CV, ML, DL, and GenAI.

Evolution of AI Applications and Technologies

Before the advent of Spatial Computing, AI had already begun its transformative journey. Early AI applications were primarily focused on solving specific, well-defined problems, such as playing chess or simple natural language understanding. These applications utilized rule-based systems, where the AI operated within a pre-determined set of guidelines.

As technology advanced, AI applications expanded to more complex tasks. This evolution was supported by the growth in computational power and the availability of large datasets, allowing for more sophisticated AI models. AI started to permeate various sectors as we have stated, from healthcare, where it assisted in diagnostic processes, to finance, where it was used for predictive analytics and risk assessment.

Categories and Types of AI Software

AI software can be broadly categorized into several types:

- **Rule-based systems:** These are early forms of AI that operate on a set of predefined rules. They are effective for structured, predictable tasks but lack the flexibility to handle complex, unstructured data.

- **ML-based systems:** ML systems learn from data, identifying patterns and making decisions with minimal human intervention. They are more adaptable than rule-based systems and can improve over time as they are exposed to more data.
- **DL-based systems:** A subset of ML, DL utilizes Neural Networks with multiple layers (hence "deep") to process data. These systems are particularly effective at handling large volumes of unstructured data, such as images and speech.
- **Hybrid systems:** These combine various AI techniques, often integrating rule-based components with ML and DL models to leverage the strengths of each approach.

NLP and Its Applications

NLP, a branch of AI, focuses on the interaction between computers and human language. It involves teaching machines to understand, interpret, and generate human language in a meaningful way. Applications of NLP are widespread, including in digital assistants (like Siri and Alexa), machine translation services (like Google Translate), and customer service chatbots.

Core Aspects of NLP

- **Language understanding:** NLP involves teaching computers to comprehend the nuances of human language, including syntax (sentence structure), semantics (meaning), and pragmatics (contextual use).
- **Language generation:** Beyond understanding, NLP also enables computers to generate coherent and contextually relevant language responses. This aspect is crucial in applications like chatbots and digital assistants.
- **Speech recognition:** NLP is not limited to text but also encompasses spoken language, enabling voice-activated systems to understand and respond to verbal commands.

Diverse Applications of NLP

- **Digital assistants:** Digital assistants like Siri, Alexa, and Google Assistant are quintessential examples of NLP in action. They interpret voice commands, understand queries, and provide responses or perform actions. The sophistication of these assistants has grown significantly, allowing for more natural and contextually aware interactions.
- **Machine translation:** Services like Google Translate exemplify NLP's application in breaking down language barriers. These services translate

text or speech from one language to another, continually improving in accuracy and fluency. While not perfect, they have become remarkably adept at providing quick and generally reliable translations.

- **Customer service chatbots:** Many businesses now employ chatbots to handle customer inquiries and provide support. These AI-driven chatbots can understand and respond to customer queries, often handling routine questions efficiently, which enhances customer service and reduces the workload on human staff.

- **Sentiment analysis:** NLP is used to analyze sentiments in text, like customer reviews or social media posts. By understanding positive, negative, or neutral sentiments, businesses can gain insights into customer opinions and reactions.

- **Content categorization and recommendation:** NLP algorithms categorize content and recommend relevant articles, products, or services to users based on their preferences and past interactions. This application is widely used in news aggregators, e-commerce platforms, and streaming services.

- **Information extraction and data mining:** NLP is crucial in extracting useful information from large volumes of unstructured text data, such as extracting key phrases, names, or specific data points from documents.

- **Speech-to-text and text-to-speech services:** These services, used in various applications from dictation software to reading aids for the visually impaired, rely on NLP to accurately convert speech to text and vice versa.

- **Language modeling and text generation:** Advanced NLP models can generate coherent and contextually relevant text, aiding in tasks ranging from writing assistance to creating entire articles or reports.

Future Prospects and Challenges

The future of NLP holds immense promise, with ongoing research and development aimed at making language processing even more nuanced and context-aware. However, there are challenges:

- **Handling ambiguity and complexity:** Human language is inherently ambiguous and complex. Developing NLP systems that can reliably interpret nuances, sarcasm, and idiomatic expressions remains a challenge.

- **Bias and fairness:** NLP models can inadvertently learn biases present in their training data, leading to biased or unfair outcomes. Addressing these biases is crucial for ethical NLP applications.

- **Multilingual and cross-cultural adaptation:** Creating NLP systems that can effectively work across multiple languages and cultural contexts is another area of ongoing development.

In conclusion, NLP serves as a cornerstone of modern AI applications, transforming how we interact with technology and how technology understands us. As NLP continues to evolve, it promises to further bridge the gap between human and machine communication, opening new horizons for accessibility, efficiency, and understanding in a digitally connected world.

CV and Its Role in AI

CV, a crucial facet of AI, is focused on giving computers the capability to interpret and make sense of the visual world. This field involves the processing of images and videos, primarily through cameras, enabling machines to identify and understand objects and scenes in a manner akin to human sight. The role of CV in AI is diverse and influential, affecting a broad spectrum of industries and applications.

Principal Functions of CV

- **Object detection and recognition:** Fundamental to CV is the ability to detect and identify objects within visual media. This includes recognizing people in photos or differentiating products in retail environments, allowing the system to accurately interpret visual data.
- **Analyzing images and videos:** CV goes beyond basic recognition, delving into comprehensive analysis. This involves contextual understanding of images, pattern recognition, and even emotion detection through facial analysis.
- **Real-time visual processing:** Many applications require Computer Vision systems to interpret and react to visual data instantly. This is especially critical in scenarios like autonomous driving, where decisions based on visual input need to be made swiftly and accurately.

CV across Various Sectors

- **Self-driving cars:** A key application of Computer Vision is in autonomous vehicles, which rely on this technology to navigate and interpret their surroundings for safe operation.

- **Healthcare applications:** In the medical field, CV assists in analyzing medical imagery for disease detection and is instrumental in patient monitoring and surgical robotics.

- **Retail industry:** Computer Vision in retail is used for inventory tracking, analyzing customer behaviors, and facilitating shopping experiences without traditional checkout processes.

- **Manufacturing and inspection:** The technology aids in quality control within manufacturing, ensuring product standards are met and identifying any defects.

- **Security and monitoring:** In security, CV is vital for facial recognition and surveillance, analyzing video footage for safety and monitoring purposes.

- **Agricultural sector:** It's transforming agriculture, helping in monitoring crops, detecting plant diseases, and predicting harvest yields.

Challenges and ethical considerations—CV, while brimming with potential, faces several challenges:

- **Ensuring precision and dependability:** The accuracy and dependability of CV systems, particularly in critical areas like autonomous vehicles or medical imaging, are of utmost importance.

- **Privacy and ethical issues:** The use of CV, especially in surveillance and facial recognition, brings up significant concerns regarding privacy and ethical practices.

- **Potential for data bias:** If trained on limited or biased data sets, CV systems may exhibit biases.

- **Computational demands:** Advanced CV tasks require substantial computational resources, which can be a constraint in some applications.

Prospects for CV

Looking ahead, the capabilities of CV are set to grow, with advancements likely in areas such as enhanced real-time analysis, better accuracy in various conditions, and more responsible usage. Merging CV with other AI domains like NLP and ML could lead to more integrated and intelligent systems that more closely mimic human interaction with the world.

In summary, CV is a foundational element of AI, driving progress and innovation across numerous fields. Its ability to process and understand visual information opens a wide array of possibilities, from improving everyday life to addressing complex challenges in different industries. As the field continues to evolve, it redefines the limits of machine perception and comprehension.

ML and DL and Their Relevance

ML and DL are key components of contemporary AI that have revolution-ized the way computers learn and make decisions. Their relevance in vari-ous sectors and applications is profound, shaping the course of technological advancement and application.

ML: A Brief Overview

ML is a subset of AI that enables computers to learn from and make predic-tions or decisions based on data. Unlike traditional programming, where rules and decisions are explicitly coded, ML algorithms learn from data, identifying patterns and making decisions with minimal human intervention.

- **Supervised Learning:** This is a common ML approach where the algo-rithm learns from labeled training data, understanding the relationship between input data and the desired output.
- **UnSupervised Learning:** In unSupervised Learning, algorithms ana-lyze and cluster unlabeled data, finding hidden patterns or intrinsic structures in the data.
- **Reinforcement Learning:** This type of learning involves an algorithm learning to make decisions by performing actions and receiving feedback from the results, akin to learning through trial and error.

DL: Expanding the Possibilities

DL, a subset of ML, involves Neural Networks with multiple layers that pro-cess data and perform tasks, mimicking the workings of the human brain. DL is particularly effective in handling large volumes of unstructured data, like images and natural language.

- **Neural Networks:** The fundamental building blocks of DL, Neural Networks, are inspired by the structure of the human brain and con-sist of interconnected nodes (neurons) that process data in a hierarchical manner.
- **Convolutional Neural Networks (CNNs):** Specialized in processing structured array data like images, CNNs are extensively used in CV for tasks like image classification and object recognition.
- **Recurrent Neural Networks (RNNs):** Ideal for processing sequential data, RNNs are used in applications involving speech recognition, NLP, and time-series analysis.

Relevance of ML and DL

In the rapidly evolving landscape of technology, ML and DL have emerged as powerful tools, revolutionizing a myriad of sectors with their ability to analyze data, predict outcomes, and automate complex tasks.

- **Data analysis and prediction:** ML algorithms are widely used for data analysis, predictive modeling, and decision-making across various industries. From financial forecasting to customer behavior analysis in retail, ML's ability to make sense of large data sets is invaluable.
- **NLP:** Both ML and DL are integral to advancing NLP, enabling more accurate and context-aware language understanding and generation.
- **Medical diagnosis and healthcare:** ML and DL have made significant strides in healthcare, aiding in disease detection, medical image analysis, and personalizing patient care.
- **Autonomous vehicles and robotics:** In the realm of autonomous vehicles and robotics, DL algorithms process and interpret sensor data, enabling machines to navigate and interact with their environment.
- **Personalization in services:** ML algorithms are behind the personalized recommendations in services like online shopping, streaming platforms, and content curation.
- **Facial recognition and security:** DL, especially through CNNs, is crucial in developing accurate facial recognition systems used in security and surveillance.

Challenges and Future Directions

Despite their transformative impact, ML and DL face challenges, such as the need for large datasets, vulnerability to biased data, and the "black box" nature of some DL models that make their decision-making processes opaque.

Future directions in ML and DL involve making algorithms more efficient, less data-hungry, and more transparent. Advances are also focused on ethical AI development, ensuring fairness and reducing biases in AI models.

In conclusion, ML and DL are not just buzzwords in the AI landscape but are core technologies driving innovation and efficiency across a spectrum of applications. Their ability to learn, adapt, and uncover insights from data is reshaping industries and opening up new frontiers in technology and human-machine interaction.

GenAI and Its Creative Potential

GenAI, a groundbreaking area within AI, involves techniques capable of creating new content or data that closely mimics human-generated output. This field has been notably advanced by the development of transformer models, alongside methods like Generative Adversarial Networks (GANs) and variational autoencoders. The transformative potential of GenAI, especially with transformers, is immense and is being leveraged in diverse fields such as art, entertainment, marketing, and more.

Core Technologies in GenAI

- **Transformers:** Initially developed for NLP tasks, transformers have proven highly effective in various generative applications. Unlike traditional models, transformers can handle sequential data, like text, more effectively due to their attention mechanisms, which allow them to consider the entire context of the data.

- **Generative Adversarial Networks (GANs):** GANs consist of two Neural Networks—the generator and the discriminator—trained in tandem. The generator creates new data, and the discriminator evaluates its authenticity, in a continuous adversarial process until the generator's output is convincingly realistic.

- **Variational autoencoders:** These are employed to generate complex outputs like images and music, by compressing data into a simpler form and then expanding it back, thereby creating new data instances.

Creative Applications and Potential

- **Art and design:** GenAI, including transformer models, is revolutionizing art and design by generating novel artworks and design concepts, thus redefining creativity's boundaries and the role of AI in creative processes.

- **Music and sound production:** In music, GenAI is capable of composing original pieces or emulating specific musical styles, offering tools for creativity and personalized music experiences.

- **Writing and content generation:** Transformers have particularly excelled in generating textual content, such as news articles, creative writing, and even coding, showcasing their versatility and potential in content creation.

- **Film and gaming**: GenAI facilitates the creation of realistic and immersive environments and characters in films and video games, streamlining production and enhancing user experiences.
- **Personalized marketing:** In marketing, GenAI can craft individualized content, improving engagement and consumer experiences.
- **Data augmentation:** For scientific research, GenAI, including transformers, can create realistic datasets, especially useful where data collection is challenging.

Challenges and Ethical Implications

The advancement of GenAI, particularly with transformers, raises several challenges and ethical issues:

- **Authenticity and originality:** Differentiating between human and AI-generated content is increasingly challenging, raising questions about the nature of originality and authenticity in the digital age.
- **Intellectual property and copyright:** The legal aspects concerning the ownership and rights of AI-generated content, especially with transformer models, are complex and still evolving.
- **Bias and misuse:** Given that transformers and other generative models learn from existing data, they can perpetuate biases. There's also the concern of their misuse in creating misleading or harmful content, like deepfakes.
- **Impact on creative fields:** While GenAI can augment human creativity, there's an ongoing debate about its potential to replace human roles in creative endeavors.

Future Directions

As transformer models and other generative techniques continue to evolve, they promise to produce more sophisticated and nuanced creative outputs. Their integration as tools for artists and creators is anticipated to grow, offering new modes of innovation and expression. However, navigating their ethical use and ensuring responsible development is essential for realizing their full potential.

In summary, GenAI, particularly with the integration of transformer models, is redefining the landscape of creative possibilities. It not only extends the capabilities of AI in generating human-like content, but also prompts important discussions about the essence of creativity and the evolving interplay between AI and human creative expression.

CV and Spatial Computing

Spatial Computing, as we have discussed, is a multifaceted field that combines physical and digital worlds. It encompasses the way computers, humans, and the physical environment interact, where digital and physical entities operate in conjunction. CV plays a critical role in Spatial Computing, providing the essential capability for machines to interpret and interact with their surroundings in real time. This integration of CV into Spatial Computing opens up a myriad of applications and functionalities.

Role of CV in Spatial Computing

- **Environmental understanding:** CV is crucial for machines to understand the environment around them. This includes recognizing objects, understanding spatial relationships, and interpreting physical layouts. In Spatial Computing, this understanding is essential for integrating digital content or information into the physical world seamlessly.

- **Object detection and recognition:** In Spatial Computing, CV is used to identify and classify objects within the environment. This capability is vital in numerous applications, from AR gaming, where virtual objects interact with real-world environments, to industrial AR, where machinery or equipment needs to be identified and monitored.

- **Depth perception and mapping:** CV algorithms are employed to assess the depth and dimensions of the physical space. This is particularly important in AR and VR, where accurate depth perception ensures that digital content is appropriately placed and sized within the real world, enhancing the realism and immersion of the experience.

- **Real-time interaction:** In Spatial Computing, interactions between users, the physical environment, and digital information must often occur in real time. CV enables this by rapidly processing visual data, allowing for immediate responses to changes in the environment or user actions.

- **Navigation and wayfinding:** In robotics and autonomous vehicles, which are part of the broader umbrella of Spatial Computing, CV is essential for navigation. It allows machines to understand their surroundings, avoid obstacles, and move through the physical world safely and efficiently.

- **Gesture and activity recognition:** In interfaces powered by Spatial Computing, CV can interpret human gestures and activities. This enables more natural and intuitive ways of interacting with digital systems, such as using hand gestures to control AR or VR applications.

Applications and Implications

- **AR and VR:** AR and VR are the most prominent examples of Spatial Computing. Here, CV ensures that virtual objects are realistically integrated into the physical world (in AR) or that virtual environments are navigable and interactive (in VR).
- **Robotics and autonomous systems:** Robots and autonomous systems use CV to interact with their environments, perform tasks, and navigate spaces, which is a key aspect of Spatial Computing.
- **Smart environments:** In smart homes and cities, Spatial Computing, aided by CV, can understand and respond to the layout of spaces and the activities of people, creating more responsive and adaptive environments.

Challenges and Future Directions

Spatial Computing, with CV at its core, faces challenges, such as ensuring accuracy in diverse and complex environments, addressing privacy concerns, and managing the computational demands of real-time processing. Future developments in this field are likely to focus on more advanced and efficient CV algorithms, better integration of AI, and resolving ethical and privacy issues, all of which will further enhance the capabilities and applications of Spatial Computing.

In summary, CV is a foundational technology in Spatial Computing, enabling machines to understand and interact with the three-dimensional world. Its integration into Spatial Computing technologies is not just enhancing user experiences and operational efficiencies but is also redefining the boundaries of how we interact with and perceive the digital and physical worlds.

Understanding the Intersection of ML/DL and Spatial Computing

ML and DL play a pivotal role in enhancing the capabilities of Spatial Computing. These advanced learning techniques enable Spatial Computing systems to process and interpret complex data, make informed decisions, and offer more natural, intuitive interactions within these blended environments.

Contributions of ML and DL to Spatial Computing

- **Interpreting physical environments:** ML and DL algorithms are adept at analyzing data from various sensors, including cameras and LiDAR, to understand and interpret physical spaces. This is especially critical in AR and VR applications, where accurate environmental interpretation is key for overlaying digital elements.

- **Object detection and classification:** Utilizing ML, particularly DL models, Spatial Computing systems can efficiently detect and classify objects within an environment. This capability is crucial for interactive applications where engagement with specific environmental features or objects is essential.

- **Forecasting and predictive analysis:** ML models are used for predictive analytics, enabling Spatial Computing systems to anticipate user actions or needs, thereby enhancing responsiveness and user experience.

- **Enhancing Natural Language interactions:** The advancement of NLP through ML and DL has greatly improved voice interactions within Spatial Computing environments, allowing for more fluid and natural voice commands in AR and VR.

- **Recognizing gestures and human activities:** DL models excel in identifying and interpreting human gestures, enabling more intuitive user interactions with digital components in Spatial Computing through simple movements.

- **Navigational intelligence:** In the context of robotics and autonomous vehicles, ML and DL are crucial for spatial awareness and path planning, ensuring safe and efficient navigation within physical spaces.

- **Customized user experiences:** Through the analysis of user data, ML algorithms can tailor experiences in Spatial Computing, from personalizing AR/VR content to adapting smart environments to individual preferences.

Practical Implications and Applications

- **Improving AR/VR Experiences:** ML and DL enhance the immersion and realism in AR and VR by refining environmental understanding, object interaction, and user interfaces.

- **Advancing robotics and autonomous systems:** These fields rely heavily on ML and DL for spatial cognition, decision-making processes, and adaptability, which are integral to Spatial Computing.

- **Optimizing smart environments:** In smart homes and cities, ML and DL enable environments to become more responsive and adaptive, understanding space and user behavior for better automation.

Challenges and Future Directions

Spatial Computing, bolstered by ML and DL, encounters challenges like ensuring data privacy, ethical AI development, computational resource management, and creating robust models for diverse environments. Future developments will likely focus on enhancing the efficiency and transparency of ML/DL models, improving data processing, and more seamlessly integrating these technologies to elevate the Spatial Computing experience.

In summary, ML and DL are foundational to the advancement of Spatial Computing, driving its ability to blend digital and physical elements effectively. Their impact is essential in transforming how we interact with and perceive our surroundings, merging the virtual and real in innovative and impactful ways.

GenAI's Role in Spatial Computing

GenAI, a branch of AI focused on creating new, human-like content, ranges from visual and auditory to textual and data forms. Known for its capability to produce new, original content, GenAI has a pivotal role in Spatial Computing. The introduction of GenAI into Spatial Computing expands the possibilities for interactions between digital and physical elements, paving the way for more nuanced, adaptive, and personalized experiences.

Contribution of GenAI in Spatial Computing

- **Realism in AR/VR:** GenAI can generate highly realistic images and environments, enhancing the immersive quality of AR and VR. This leads to experiences where the distinction between the virtual and the real is increasingly subtle.
- **On-the-fly content generation:** GenAI enables the creation of dynamic content in Spatial Computing, tailored to user interactions and environmental changes. This includes generating personalized digital artifacts in AR or entire environments in VR.

- **Real-world environment simulation:** It is capable of simulating real-life scenarios, beneficial for training, education, and gaming in Spatial Computing. This allows for the generation of diverse and lifelike scenarios that adapt in real time.
- **Personalized experiences:** In Spatial Computing settings, GenAI can craft experiences unique to each user, generating content that resonates with individual preferences or specific interaction histories.
- **Predictive models in smart spaces:** GenAI can anticipate and model the usage of physical spaces and objects in smart environments, leading to smarter, more proactive system responses.
- **Evolving art and design:** GenAI facilitates the creation of interactive, evolving art and design pieces within Spatial Computing that can respond to environmental inputs or viewer interactions.

Challenges and Future Directions

The fusion of GenAI with Spatial Computing brings its set of challenges, including ethical considerations around generated content, the necessity for unbiased and reliable AI models, and the computational intensity required for real-time content generation in intricate environments. Future advancements are likely to focus on developing more efficient, ethical GenAI solutions, enhancing their integration within Spatial Computing, and exploring novel applications that stretch the limits of this synergy.

The integration of GenAI into Spatial Computing significantly enhances the realm, offering more immersive, tailored, and dynamic interactions within combined digital-physical environments. This capability to generate context-responsive content revolutionizes how technology is perceived and interacted with, progressively blurring the lines between virtual and real spaces. As these technologies evolve, the relationship between GenAI and Spatial Computing is set to redefine our digital experiences, merging virtual and physical realities in ways previously unimagined.

Hardware Companies Leveraging AI

Spatial Computing has gained significant traction, and various companies are at the forefront of this technological evolution. Notably, many hardware companies are leveraging AI to enhance their offerings, particularly in terms of GPU acceleration and other advanced hardware solutions. Let's explore some of these companies and their contributions, categorized by functionality.

NVIDIA

Functionality: GPU Acceleration and AI Processing

Contributions: NVIDIA is a leader in graphics processing unit (GPU) technology, which is crucial for both AI and Spatial Computing. Their GPUs are not just for rendering complex graphics, but also for accelerating AI tasks, including those in Spatial Computing. NVIDIA's CUDA platform is a key enabler, allowing for parallel processing that significantly speeds up AI algorithms, essential for real-time Spatial Computing applications. The company also develops AI-specific hardware like the NVIDIA DGX systems and Tegra processors, which are used in autonomous vehicles and smart devices, essential components of the Spatial Computing ecosystem.

Intel

Functionality: CPU and AI Chip Development

Contributions: Intel, traditionally known for its central processing units (CPUs), has expanded into AI hardware. Their AI-focused chips, such as the Intel Nervana Neural Network Processors, are designed to efficiently handle DL tasks. Intel's RealSense technology, which includes depth-sensing cameras, is particularly relevant for Spatial Computing, providing vital data for real-time 3D mapping and object recognition.

Qualcomm

Functionality: Mobile and IoT Device AI Integration

Contributions: Qualcomm is a major player in mobile processors and has integrated AI capabilities into its Snapdragon series. These processors are widely used in smartphones and IoT devices, which are key interfaces in Spatial Computing. Qualcomm's AI Engine and dedicated Hexagon DSP (Digital Signal Processor) provide advanced AI processing capabilities in energy-efficient ways, crucial for mobile and edge devices used in AR, VR, and smart environments.

AMD

Functionality: GPU and CPU for AI Tasks

Contributions: AMD, known for both CPUs and GPUs, is increasingly integrating AI capabilities into its hardware. Their Radeon GPUs are not only for gaming and graphics, but also support AI processing, beneficial for Spatial Computing applications that require intensive graphics and parallel processing capabilities.

Apple

Functionality: Integrated AI in Consumer Devices

Contributions: Apple's integration of AI into its hardware, particularly with the development of the Neural Engine in its A-series and M-series chips, is notable. These chips power a range of devices from iPhones to Macs and are essential for AR applications, which are a significant part of Spatial Computing. Apple's focus on combining AI with user-friendly design makes their devices an integral part of the Spatial Computing landscape.

ARM

Functionality: AI-Enabled Processor Designs

Contributions: ARM designs processors that are widely used in mobile devices and IoT applications. Their Cortex CPUs and Mali GPUs are designed to be power-efficient, which is crucial for mobile AR/VR devices. ARM's technology is instrumental in enabling AI processing in small, portable devices, a key component in the Spatial Computing ecosystem.

These companies demonstrate the diverse ways in which hardware is being optimized for AI, a critical element in advancing Spatial Computing. By focusing on GPU acceleration, AI-specific chips, and integrated AI processing capabilities, these companies are not only enhancing the performance and capabilities of Spatial Computing systems, but also shaping the future landscape of how digital and physical worlds converge. As Spatial Computing continues to grow, the contributions of these hardware companies will likely become even more pivotal, driving innovation and enabling new applications in this dynamic field.

Software Companies with AI-Driven Solutions

These software companies, through their AI-driven solutions, are at the forefront of advancing Spatial Computing. By providing powerful development platforms, AI integration tools, and cloud services, they are enabling the creation of more immersive, intelligent, and interactive Spatial Computing experiences. Their contributions are not only vital in shaping the current landscape of Spatial Computing but also in paving the way for future innovations in this dynamic field. As Spatial Computing continues to evolve, the role of these software giants in integrating AI into the digital-physical convergence will become increasingly significant.

Unity Technologies

Functionality: Game Engine and Real-Time 3D Development

Contributions: Unity is renowned for its game engine, widely used for creating AR and VR content. It has evolved into a comprehensive platform for real-time 3D development, crucial for Spatial Computing. Unity's engine supports AI-driven functionalities like ML, NLP, and CV, enabling developers to create sophisticated, interactive Spatial Computing applications. The platform also facilitates the integration of AI models and simulations, making it a go-to tool for AR/VR developers and creators.

Unreal Engine (Epic Games)

Functionality: Advanced 3D Visualization and Interactive Experiences

Contributions: Unreal Engine, developed by Epic Games, is another leading platform in the realm of Spatial Computing. Known for its high-fidelity graphics, the engine is instrumental in developing immersive VR and AR experiences. Unreal Engine incorporates AI functionalities, such as AI-driven character behavior and environment simulation, enhancing the realism and interactivity of Spatial Computing applications.

Google (with TensorFlow)

Functionality: ML and AI Development

Contributions: Google's TensorFlow is a powerful open-source platform for ML, widely used in AI applications, including those in Spatial Computing. TensorFlow facilitates the development of sophisticated ML models that can be integrated into AR and VR applications, enabling features like object recognition, gesture analysis, and predictive analytics.

Amazon Web Services (AWS)

Functionality: Cloud Computing and AI Services

Contributions: AWS offers a range of cloud-based AI services that are applicable in Spatial Computing. Services like Amazon SageMaker enable developers to build, train, and deploy ML models quickly, which can be integrated into Spatial Computing applications for enhanced interactivity and smart functionalities.

Microsoft (with Azure AI)

Functionality: AI Solutions and Cloud Computing

Contributions: Microsoft's Azure AI provides a suite of AI tools and services that support the development of Spatial Computing applications. Azure's AI capabilities, including CV, speech recognition, and decision-making algorithms, can be integrated into AR, VR, and mixed-reality applications to create more intelligent and responsive experiences.

Adobe

Functionality: Creative and Design Software

Contributions: Adobe, known for its creative software suite, has been integrating AI (through its Adobe Sensei platform) into its products. These AI-driven tools are useful in the creation of assets and experiences for Spatial Computing, offering functionalities like image recognition, enhanced graphics rendering, and content personalization.

AI-Driven Decision-Making in Spatial Computing

One of the most important areas where AI touches Spatial Computing is in decision-making. AI-driven decision-making in Spatial Computing represents a sophisticated interplay between technology, data analysis, and real-time responsiveness to the physical environment. This integration is crucial for various applications, from AR to autonomous vehicles, smart environments, and beyond. Understanding the intricacies of this process reveals the complexity and potential of AI in Spatial Computing.

Real-Time Data Processing and Analysis

At the core of AI-driven decision-making in Spatial Computing is the ability to process and analyze data in real time. Spatial Computing devices, equipped with an array of sensors, continually gather vast amounts of data about their surroundings. This data can include visual inputs from cameras, spatial information from LiDAR or depth sensors, auditory data from microphones, and more.

AI algorithms process this multi-sensor data to construct a comprehensive understanding of the physical space. They can recognize objects, understand spatial relationships, and even interpret human gestures and expressions. This real-time processing is essential for making informed decisions based on current environmental conditions.

Contextual Understanding and Responsiveness

Another crucial aspect is the AI system's ability to understand the context of the environment it is operating in. Contextual understanding means recognizing not just the physical layout of a space, but also its purpose, the activities typically performed there, and the presence and behavior of people and objects within it.

For instance, in an AR application, the AI must decide what information is relevant to the user at a specific moment and location. In a museum, it might provide detailed information about artworks; in a retail store, it might offer product recommendations or navigation help.

Predictive Analytics and Anticipatory Actions

AI in Spatial Computing often employs predictive analytics to anticipate future scenarios and act proactively. This is particularly evident in autonomous vehicles, where AI systems must predict the actions of pedestrians, cyclists, and other vehicles to navigate safely and efficiently.

Predictive analytics involves analyzing past and present data to make educated guesses about future events. In Spatial Computing, this means understanding regular patterns and anomalies in environmental data, enabling the AI to make more accurate decisions and take anticipatory actions.

Interactive and Adaptive Systems

Spatial Computing AI systems are interactive and adaptive, constantly learning from new data and user interactions. This adaptability allows the system to improve over time, offering more personalized and accurate responses to environmental stimuli.

In smart-home environments, for instance, AI systems learn the preferences and habits of the inhabitants, adjusting lighting, temperature, and other settings automatically to optimize comfort and energy efficiency.

Challenges in AI-Driven Decision-Making

Despite these advancements, AI-driven decision-making in Spatial Computing faces several challenges:

- **Data privacy and security:** The extensive data collection necessary for Spatial Computing raises concerns about privacy and data security. Ensuring that user data is protected and used ethically is a significant challenge.

- **Complexity of real-world environments:** The real world is unpredictable and complex. AI systems must be robust enough to handle this complexity and make reliable decisions even in novel or chaotic situations.

- **Algorithmic bias and fairness:** There is a risk of bias in AI decision-making, particularly if the training data is not representative or contains inherent biases. Ensuring fairness and impartiality in AI decisions is crucial.

- **Human-AI interaction:** Designing AI systems that interact effectively and intuitively with humans is challenging. The system must be able to interpret human intentions correctly and respond in ways that are understandable and helpful.

Overall, AI-driven decision-making in Spatial Computing is a dynamic and evolving field, marked by significant advancements and complex challenges. As this technology continues to develop, it holds immense potential for transforming how we interact with the world around us, making our environments more responsive, efficient, and attuned to our needs. Next, we focus on how AI in Spatial Computing produces business benefits.

Business Benefits of AI in Spatial Computing

Expanding further on the critical role of AI in Spatial Computing, we need to now explore its tangible business benefits. What does this convergence mean for business and how can businesses benefit from its current integration today, while keeping their eyes on the fast evolution of how AI and Spatial Computing are converging?

Some of the tangible business benefits of AI in Spatial Computing include:

- **Improved customer experiences in retail and e-commerce:** Aside from chatbots, AI in Spatial Computing provides a more robust experience for customer support in retail and e-commerce experiences. E-commerce is transforming into virtual storefronts, where shops create a digital twin of their retail locations online. Obsess, an experimental e-commerce platform, uses GenAI to design virtual storefronts with increased efficiency and generate dynamic content at scale.[1] Virtual chatbots are upgraded into a virtual, life-like person that can tailor personalized responses to shoppers' preferences in real time.

  In physical retail locations, AI in Spatial Computing plays a different role. Personalization is more possible online but physical retail stores can use AI in Spatial Computing to bring that personalization to customers in-store, bridging the gap between their digital and physical shopping habits. AI in Spatial Computing in-store can timestamp customers' journey in physical retail locations, creating a full-profile view of the customer. Although not everyone has a Spatial Computing device yet, smartphones are getting close. As wearables with Spatial Computing-enabled technology come to market, retailers can use these devices along with AI and datasets to guide customers through new in-store shopping experiences, guide them to try different products or optimize their shopping time based on preferences like concierge services from in-store attendants, solo shopping, and window shoppers to those who are in-and-out.

- **Enhanced training and simulations in healthcare and education:** The saying practice makes perfect is true for anyone but especially holds true for healthcare professionals. Learning the human body and a variety of situations is the only way for practitioners to improve. From using cadavers to advanced simulations using Virtual Reality and simulation labs, healthcare training and education have improved by leaps and bounds. Add AI in Spatial Computing to the mix and healthcare providers have a whole new set of training opportunities and education.

  AI in Spatial Computing isn't just for learning and practicing before performing. AI in Spatial Computing helps surgeons assess their operations. The role of AI in Spatial Computing for healthcare education is to improve speed, quality, or both from beginners to seasoned practitioners. AI in Spatial Computing when integrated into current healthcare workflows educates healthcare workers in real-time, using massive amounts of data and learning to help physicians identify conditions faster.[2] AI in Spatial Computing combined with connected devices allows practitioners to see parts of the human body they couldn't before, such as new angles in the lungs, which inform procedures and diagnosis.

- **Increased efficiency in manufacturing and logistics:** AI in Spatial Computing has the potential to revolutionize manufacturing. At present, many plants operate with technology, robotics, sensors, and data capture. Alongside their human counterparts, AI in Spatial Computing can teach operators in real time. AI in Spatial Computing removes the need for outdated Human Machine Interfaces because it can learn from the operator at a specific station as well as use CV via the cameras in the plant and other sensors to identify issues on the line, product defects, and other quality concerns. AI in Spatial Computing can report the relevant information back to its operator to make adjustments in real time. AI in Spatial Computing in manufacturing and logistics, when implemented properly, reduces waste, increases time to market, and improves operator safety at scale.

- **Creative applications in gaming and entertainment:** Gaming and entertainment industries are primed for AI in Spatial Computing. From their users to the adoption of new technology, AI in Spatial Computing offers creative applications to the ways we watch, play, and game. Switching from the use of joysticks and keypads to gaze and gesture controls is one way AI in Spatial Computing offers creative applications for developers. AI in Spatial Computing becomes interesting in the gamification of real-world events, such as creating digital twins of basketball players in a live game and fans being able to interact in the basketball game through their spatial computer.

  AI in Spatial Computing allows developers to create games 3D-first instead of trying to make a 2D-designed game fit into Spatial Computing. The ability to take advantage of real-world environments, incorporate AI to speed up the development of objects and scenes, and the ability to create spatially with the power of a Spatial Computer will create whole new industries for developing games, making movies, musical performances, and other entertainment.

- **Advancements in the agriculture industry:** The agriculture industry is not new to technology. Tractors and farming equipment are loaded with sensors that track the spread of seeds, and estimate the quality of the plant based on the soil, and other such indicators. John Deere revealed a fully autonomous tractor at CES in 2022.[3] AI in Spatial Computing is a key advancement for these connected vehicles, sensors, and devices for enhancing precision farming like detecting pests, plant health, and resource allocation optimization. The advanced spatial visualization of AI in Spatial Computing allows farmers to gain new insights and identify new patterns from complex agricultural data.

  In real estate, AI in Spatial Computing offers a wide variety of use cases from digital twins of buildings and homes to placing furniture or digitally flipping a house before construction.

- **Innovations in automotive and transportation industries:** AI in Spatial Computing offers a transition from static, 2D maps for users and transportation planners alike. Integrating AI in Spatial Computing into vehicles via Heads Up Display (HUD) like the BMW 7 Series or the Jaguar XF incorporate holographic displays that can tell the driver anything from traffic conditions, gear shift points to assist in shifting, g-meters in a lateral turn, or, when offroading, steering angles and pitch. AI in Spatial Computing is an example of an activity most of us use every day, but layered with information and assistance we didn't have access to before.

  AI in Spatial Computing for transportation planners takes data from sensors on the road, connected cars, and other connected data points in infrastructure and uses that to plan routes, predict traffic, and account for road conditions. AI in Spatial Computing applies to bus transportation, using spatial analytics to predict demand for various bus routes. For aircraft, AI in Spatial Computing can check planes for damage from birds, lighting, or other occurrences faster and more efficiently than human, pre-flight checks. AI in Spatial Computing reduces the time for inspection and provides real-time reporting. In one case, damage inspection times went from 30 minutes to 3 minutes using an AI in Spatial Computing solution.[4]

To help illustrate this, we have identified two case studies of how companies have harnessed AI in Spatial Computing with successful metrics and clear benefits.

Lockheed Martin

Lockheed Martin, an aerospace and defense company, used Spatial Computing to reduce the amount of time it took to train employees in one of their projects. Lockheed Martin used the Microsoft HoloLens 1 combined with Scope AR's software to reduce training time by 85%[5] and also achieved a 93% reduction in costs on one part of the manufacturing process for the Orion space vehicle when they implemented Augmented Reality aids. What once took eight shifts of eight hours each was reduced to six hours via Microsoft HoloLens and Scope AR's Worklink. Those metrics are often touted as a clear example of how Spatial Computing can achieve cost-reducing benefits for a business as well as help optimize process flows in highly complicated manufacturing projects.

NBA Launchpad

The National Basketball Association's initiative to pilot emerging technologies for fan experiences at home and in NBA arenas has invested in multiple companies focused on AI and Spatial Computing to drive innovation in basketball. The companies in the NBA Launchpad initiative range from CV and ML to generate player tracking data to using spatial data to create 3D-sound experiences for low-vision fans. Action Audio, the company behind the 3D sound technology, uses spatial data from a ball-monitoring CV system to design sound experiences.[6] The NBA is an example of an entertainment and sports company using AI and Spatial Computing to enhance player well-being, build immersive experiences for fans, use technology to enhance their digital library of 75 years' worth of content, and uncover new insights.

The NBA also uses 3D optical tracking technology called Hawk-Eye by Sony. Hawk-Eye is made up of four cameras with 4K resolution that should operate at 120 frames per second. The goal of Hawk-Eye is to assist referees in real time. The cameras capture the players' data like positional data of their hands and apply it to the rules of goaltending and the laws of physics.[7] It outputs a yes-no response, which is sent in real time to the referees via audio or wristwatch. This version of Hawk-Eye was deployed for the 2023–2024 basketball calendar.

Enhanced Decision-Making with AI and Spatial Computing

Through AI's role in Spatial Computing, users can also unlock other business benefits, one of them having enhanced decision-making through the use of Spatial Computing applications.

Both Irena and Cathy's teams have become early developers for the Apple Vision Pro and are using the latest tools to create new AI-driven Spatial Computing tools that enhance decision-making through spatially powered tools.

Two important ways that decision-making is being enhanced via these tools include:

- **Real-time data analysis and insights:** AI and Spatial Computing process, interpret, and visualize data in a more intelligent and context-aware manner than traditional systems. Real-time data analysis comes from AI ML and DL's ability to analyze large amounts of data and identify patterns quickly. Spatial Computing composition of geospatial integration and spatial awareness via CV provides analysis of data in the context of physical locations and objects. These are some of the features of AI and Spatial Computing that are valuable for a variety of industries.

- **Predictive analytics for improved planning:** Insights into future trends, customer behaviors, and world events come from AI and Spatial Computing. The convergence of these technologies combined with diverse data sets, updated AI models, and spatial context will empower organizations to make newly informed decisions and their ability to respond to challenges in real time.

While using these tools to enhance the decisions made and optimize processes, serious ethical considerations must be discussed regarding AI-driven Spatial Computing. From addressing privacy concerns (related to a user's time, location, data input and output, gestures, biometrics, and beyond) to ensuring the fairness and transparency of AI Algorithms, which in itself is no easy feat given the black box nature of many of the models used to train data sets. We will expand on our concerns in further detail in a future chapter, but we want to make sure that, as a reader, you keep in mind that these considerations should be at the forefront of how you decide to implement AI-drive Spatial Computing into your business.

A Look at the Regulatory Environment

AI has already been met with scrutiny regarding biases in data, lack of diversity of thought on AI teams, lack of standardization in the industry and, globally, missing ethical considerations and a general lag in regulations addressing Artificial Intelligence technologies and application.

First, we must look at the current regulatory landscape in the context of AI and Spatial Computing.

Here's a brief overview of some of the existing regulations and guidelines.

- An October 2023 Executive Order on the Safe, Secure, and Trustworthy Development and Use of Artificial Intelligence
- The European Union General Data Protection Regulation (GDPR)
- The proposal for an EU Artificial Intelligence Act

Some of the emerging regulations we see on the horizon include:

- Privacy laws and geospatial data
- Geospatial Data Infrastructure regulations
- Virtual Air Rights
- Autonomous vehicle regulations

The regulatory tensions around AI and in the future around AI-driven Spatial Computing could potentially impact businesses in the following ways:

- What data a company is allowed to collect
- What data a company is allowed to feed into its AI and Spatial Computing System

- The type of data collected and trained to remove biases
- Transparency options for customers in how their data is used to train AI and feed Spatial Computing Systems

Future Prospects and Preparation

In order to further our analysis and discussion for this book, we need to now look into the future prospects of AI in Spatial Computing and how businesses can prepare for continued AI-driven transformation. In 2024, AI will continue to be an important priority for businesses, but since Spatial Computing will start to enter the business conversation, it's important to consider both AI and Spatial Computing's convergence in the business context and business outlook of the rest of this decade. Here are some ways businesses can start preparing:

- Assess the skill sets of their teams. Assess your team to see if they have what it takes to apply AI and Spatial Computing to the business. If they don't, it may be time for training or to partner with a Spatial Computing company.
- Look for opportunities to embrace 3D and AI inside the company and in customer-facing scenarios.
- Rethink your data. How is it captured and stored? Is it AI-friendly?
- Assess your systems and infrastructure. AI and Spatial Computing will make many of our current systems obsolete. Conduct an assessment to see what infrastructure will support AI and Spatial Computing and what is on its way out.
- Start with a pilot. Don't try to change everything in the company at once. Pick one area to try Spatial Computing. Use AI and Spatial Computing to capture the process, identify learning opportunities, and assess what new metrics can be captured from the pilot.

Conclusions: Looking Ahead

In this chapter, we explored the evolution of AI and its role in transforming today's business landscape. We then looked at how AI functions in Spatial Computing as well as the companies leveraging these technologies.

We presented the business benefits of AI in Spatial Computing using real-life use cases from Lockheed Martin and the NBA. These are only two examples of companies expanding their offerings, enhancing their quality, and increasing speed using AI and Spatial Computing.

While the regulatory environment has catching up to do, we will no doubt see it evolve as more use cases for AI and Spatial Computing present themselves.

We can't emphasize enough the pivotal role AI plays in the Spatial Computing era. Despite our enthusiasm, we also had to include a discussion on the ethical and regulatory aspects of how these technologies are reshaping businesses through Spatial Computing.

In future chapters, we hope to present a forward-looking perspective on the ongoing AI revolution and its potential implications for the business world.

CHAPTER 2

The Evolution of a New Era of Spatial Computing

S patial Computing has far-reaching applications beyond AR and VR. It offers a new way to process data and return that information to its users. Spatial Computing does display graphics in 3D form and makes all surfaced spatial interfaces, but even more important is its ability to think and learn from its surroundings spatially via Artificial Intelligence, and for the first time, makes machines learn from what's happening around them instead of humans having to learn how to interact with machines. In order to understand these implications, we first must deep dive into the origin of Spatial Computing and how this method of processing data and the capability of machines to see the world originated.

Understanding the Foundations

Spatial Computing can trace its origins back to the work done in AR, VR, and AI. It is through Spatial Computing that these technologies converge in a meaningful and useful way. While AI had been evolutionary for a few decades, it jumped into its revolutionary era in 2022 with the release of OpenAI's ChatGPT. AR and VR have been in development for several decades as well, and to some, both are in their evolutionary phase waiting for their killer app moment. That is why the current moment we are living through is so significant as it pertains to the convergence of all three.

As mentioned in the Introduction, the earliest academic definition of *Spatial Computing* was penned by Simon Greenwold in 2003. Greenwold's idea that machines can remember and manipulate real objects and spaces with a human in a human-like way will change how we think about computers and machines in our lives. Work and play will forever be changed and Spatial Computing-enabled machines enter our offices, manufacturing facilities, and homes.

Spatial Computers that understand the significance of data, objects, and spaces to their users will transform how we experience entertainment, understand stories, and make decisions. Spatial Computers will see our world in new ways. New metrics don't have to be created for Spatial Computing. Instead, Spatial Computing will display data already collected in new ways. This leads to reductions in waste, changes in output, and other metrics that we already strive for.

From Science Fiction to Business Reality

While she worked at Magic Leap, author Hackl described Spatial Computing as a new form of computing that uses AI and CV to seamlessly blend digital content into someone's reality. Noted in a 2018 article by Magic Leap's CEO at the time, Rony Abovitz, he viewed the Spatial Computing device and system holistically as a co-processor to the human brain. Abovitz described a platform of the future focused on human-centered AI, understanding one's environment, and context awareness.[1] While not at odds with Greenwold's definition, this take, and others like it, focus on the ability of the computer to place virtual elements in the physical world rather than their ability to bring physical elements into a virtual world.

A post by Chris Lee on the Amazon Web Services (AWS) blog "Chris Lee of Amazon Web Services," similarly defined *Spatial Computing* as "the combination of the virtual and physical worlds."[2] Bill Vass of AWS defined it as "the potential digitization (or virtualization, or digital twin) of all objects, systems, machines, people, their interactions and environments."[3] While Lee's post focuses on the potential use of Spatial Computing as a means of generating and experiencing new kinds of entertainment media, Vass's post focuses on Spatial Computing as a collaborative experience medium.

Microsoft similarly presented Spatial Computing as an extension of the self via devices being aware of their surroundings and representing themselves digitally. Human-centered AI is a missing component in their Spatial Computing concept. Instead, Microsoft promotes Spatial Computing as the next stage in human-robot interaction, bringing the conversation back to Greenwold's focus on Spatial Computing as fundamentally being a new kind of relationship between humans and computers.

Apple and Meta both focus their branding of Spatial Computing in language similar to Greenwold's, but that focuses on the ability of Spatial Computing platforms to allow the presence of other humans, whether remote humans represented virtually or co-present humans viewable within the display.

A working definition of *Spatial Computing* that everyone agreed on had not been arrived at yet, so we decided in mid-2023 that we needed to craft a working definition for use in the business world.

As mentioned in the Introduction, the working definition of Spatial Computing that we, the authors, present is the following:

> Spatial Computing is an evolving 3D-centric form of computing that, at its core, uses AI, CV, and extended reality to blend virtual experiences into the physical world that break free from screens and make all surfaces spatial interfaces. It allows humans, devices, computers, robots, and virtual beings to navigate through computing in 3D space. It ushers in a new paradigm for human-to-human interaction as well as human–computer interaction, enhancing how we visualize, simulate, and interact with data in physical or virtual locations and expanding computing beyond the confines of the screen into everything you can see, experience, and know.
>
> Spatial Computing allows us to navigate the world alongside robots, drones, cars, virtual assistants, and beyond and is not limited to just one technology or just one device. It is a mix of software, hardware, and information that allows humans and technology to connect in new ways ushering in a new form of computing that could be even more impactful than personal computing and mobile computing have been to society.

How Spatial Computing Works

AI's Critical Role in Spatial Computing

AI has been behind AR for years. The recognition of the environment that is necessary for even basic AR applications is driven by CV. This is true down to placing an object on a surface—which requires the program to understand where the surface is and what its being a surface means, at least within the context of that program.

However, CV isn't exactly the same as computer learning and AI. AI helps to improve the accuracy and speed of object and scene recognition and helps the program to do more with that information, like powering hand tracking. These systems also allow virtual objects to behave believably in the physical world. For example, a platform that had only basic surface recognition might allow a user to place a basic 3D model on a desk, but that would be the end of the interaction. A more powerful platform allows users to place a virtual character on a physical desk and allow that character to believably roam the surface and potentially even interact with other objects in the area.

AR games by Niantic present a good example of this. Pokémon Go was released in 2016. The digital characters could be seen in the real world through the camera feed, but they weren't highly interactive. A basic understanding of the user's environment had some influence on which Pokémon appeared where, but once they appeared they didn't interact with the environment in meaningful ways.

Peridot, also by Niantic, was released in 2023 and largely flipped the script. Rather than different environments resulting in different largely non-reactive virtual characters, a single virtual character interacts with different physical environments. Not only can the program tell water from grass, but it can also identify flowers and animals—each eliciting a different interaction from the virtual pet.

Computer Vision and AR combined with AI are three important components to creating working Spatial Computing. CV allows computers to "see" their real-world environment through cameras and sensors. CV Systems allow machines to recognize the spatial context of the user. When used in conjunction with AI, machines with CV can start to predict, react, and make decisions in reference to the human with whom it is interacting.

Think about a manufacturing line. Manufacturing plants are the epitome of connected humans and machines. Sensors, cameras, robots, and humans all work together to create a final product. Imagine an operator equipped with a spatial computer. They no longer have a need for a physical touch screen to operate their station. The spatial computer monitors the operator's time on a part and the output and connects that information with the rest of the line in the plant. The spatial computer can give real-time information to the operator on how to adjust their station to improve every part.

AR is the component that allows digital elements to be overlaid in the physical world. It is with AR that machines and their users can start to understand the spatial context of virtual objects and how they relate to physical and digital environments.

AI Recognizes Our Hand Gestures and Body Language

Similarly, many Spatial Computing applications need to be able to recognize the presence of a human face or body. Some systems use trackers and sensors to pick up our body movements to render users in virtual, full-body representations, such as communicating remotely with friends and co-workers.

As advanced Spatial Computing applications work with gesture control, AI is also required to identify and interpret the movements of the fingers. Nuanced finger tracking can be used for the navigation of menus and for basic commands. However, it can also be used, paired with a Spatial Computing platform's understanding of the physical and virtual environment, to allow natural interactions between a physical hand and a virtual object.

Interactions like these are already possible, but require special gloves that track the fingers and report back to the Spatial Computing platform. The upside of these products is that they can also provide haptic feedback that allows the wearer to literally feel virtual objects. The drawback of these products is that the additional hardware, in addition to often being bulky, is prohibitively expensive for the average consumer. However, these applications do have their use cases, primarily in enterprise and research.

Conversational Navigation

Some platforms do not operate with hand gestures but with voice commands. Many such systems recognize a set (and very limited) list of commands. With varying degrees of complexity, the user has to say a command perfectly clearly using the right words in the right order, almost like a magic spell. As these technologies advance, applications will be more capable of understanding our meaning even if we use the wrong words, have an accent, or say them while flustered or frustrated.

This might be the area of Spatial Computing in which the recent developments in AI have been most beneficial. Much of the recent progress in AI has been in a specific type of AI called the "Large Language Model"—a system of ML in which the system analyzes language inputs to generate its own language outputs. Taking into consideration all of those definitions of Spatial Computing that posit it as a relationship between people and computers, it makes sense that humans and computers will need a better way to communicate. Large Language Models are fueling that communication.

While many of those reading this will remember learning the standard menu system first for desktop computers, then for mobile devices, maybe then for VR headsets and AR glasses. Even before the modern computer was invented, people have dreamed of a more natural way to interact with what they conceived would be computers. We know our way around the devices that we use every day, but humans are social animals. Most of us feel that there is something missing in all of the endless typing, clicking, tapping, and scrolling.

Amazon is already introducing us to this world with their Echo Frames, part of the Alexa ecosystem, allowing us to take the voice-controlled AI Assistant everywhere we go. Amazon Echo can act as a touch-free interface to our phones and audio media like music and podcasts. When it's patched into our increasingly connected homes, it can set the thermostat, control the lights, and answer that never-ending question of whether we locked the door before we left.

For most people, voice commands will be a convenient and natural way to communicate to Spatial Computing devices and applications. However, there are some situations in which there are simply no alternatives. Later in this chapter, we'll discuss the expanding role of Spatial Computing in fields like manufacturing—including situations in which a user's hands are far too busy to serve as inputs through systems like touch pads or gesture tracking.

Further, AI-assisted voice commands won't just be how people navigate Spatial Computing devices and experiences. They will also be how people navigate AI itself. AI gives us access to seemingly limitless information. Many people are underwhelmed by AI chatbots on web browsers, but this isn't an issue with AI. This only happens when companies limit the potential of AI by forcing users to interact with it through outdated control systems.

Our earliest interactions with ML and AI involved feeding it information. We're now in a period where AI can give back that information (though still not tell us much that we didn't already know), but it can also generate its own art and ideas. Mustafa Suleyman calls this coming period, "Interactive AI."

In 2010, Suleyman co-founded the AI company DeepMind. When Deep-Mind became a subsidiary of Google, Suleyman transitioned to Google's vice president of AI Product Management and AI Policy—a position that he held until co-founding Inflection AI. Inflection AI developed Pi—a personal AI on iOS devices that helps users stay focused and organized or just chats with them when they need to vent or bounce ideas off a soundboard.

The era of interactive AI, which is just now dawning, will see AI that can engage in meaningful dialogue with us. We won't just tell it what we want, and it won't just tell us what someone else said. Instead, AI and humans will work together combining our strengths and even our creativity to find solutions to new problems and unlock new levels of artistic expression and entertainment.

Beyond Conversation

A few months after Apple announced its Spatial Computing headset, it announced the iPhone 15 and the next version of the Apple Watch. The Apple Watch is the most personal computing device that many people own. In fact, it knows them better than they know themselves by notifying them of how well they sleep, how their hearts function, and more. A device like this exists not as a standalone health monitor, but as one star in a constellation of other connected devices. It is a sign of things to come.

Technologies like these, as well as neural interfaces, will make our interactions with technology easier—beyond natural—and even more personal and powerful.

Object and Scene Generation

AI that grants Spatial Computing platforms the ability to see and understand physical objects and scenes is part of the "ML" aspect of AI that researchers have been working toward for almost a hundred years. However, a new kind of AI has grabbed the world's attention in the past year or so. That's Generative AI—AI that doesn't understand what's already there, but rather creates its own content.

This branch of AI is rapidly evolving from text input generating text output to text input generating image and video output on to some applications that now allow us to speak 3D virtual objects into existence in our virtual worlds. This kind of software promises to further democratize the development of Spatial Computing experiences by allowing people with no history of coding or design to craft their own objects and environments.

A person's immediate thought might be the entertainment space, as individual users are able to create their own fantastic immersive experiences and games. That is a powerful use case, certainly, but consider an expert in a particular field who can directly apply their expertise to a training module or immersive lesson plan without needing to learn development tools or pay for expert designers.

Of course, expert designers and experienced developers will still be needed—at least for the foreseeable future. Most of the games that we play and movies that we watch will still be created by "AAA" studios (though these studios too will use AI to lessen workloads and speed up production times). The promise here is for people like educators and small business owners (who don't have the budget to hire developers or the time to learn code) will be able to create something memorable for their students or employees.

Spatial Navigation for Autonomous Vehicles, Drones, and Robots

Spatial Computing isn't just for humans. We have created all sorts of artificial agents like robots, drones, and even vehicles. However, these all still require a human pilot—even if that pilot isn't onboard. AI powered by Spatial Computing is approaching the stage at which they can take the reins.

There are two kinds of sensors at play here. One is very similar to the hardware and software that powers the AR experience. Cameras serve as the agent's eyes detecting markings on pavement, changing traffic signals, and even dynamic obstacles in the road like other cars, debris, and pedestrians.

The other kind of sensor is unlike any kind of sense that we humans possess. It's the ability of an intelligent agent to pick up signals from other connected devices as well as from internet and satellite sources.

Autonomous vehicles: While driverless vehicles are going through their paces as we speak, including select cities offering autonomous taxi services, there is still a lot of work that needs to go into these systems for autonomous vehicles.

The modern traffic system was designed for human drivers. Conventional road markings confuse autonomous vehicles. Not all roads may have reliable markings or markings that are visible year-round. Further, in 2017, artist James Bridle demonstrated that autonomous vehicles could be "trapped" by drawing lines around them.[4] While self-driving cars have gotten a bit smarter in the last few years, we can only predict that people will keep trying to outsmart them. And, when it comes to vehicle safety, autonomous cars don't just need to work—they need to be foolproof.

Similarly, while autonomous vehicles sensing the presence of other vehicles, pedestrians, and intelligent roadside infrastructure is promising and possible, these technologies will have to be institutionalized not only in the vehicles themselves, but also in roadway maintenance. This too has its potential problems. While a streetlamp broadcasting its position to a network for driverless cars to prevent collisions is one thing, will people opt into a similar solution if it means giving away their position—even anonymously? And what about people who don't carry phones or people who carry more than one phone?

There is also room to ask questions about the AI behind autonomous vehicles and how it might make the difficult decisions that human drivers sometimes have to make. There are endless "trolley problems" that we can pose in reference to autonomous vehicles. If a pedestrian steps into the street before an autonomous vehicle has cleared an intersection, will the autonomous vehicle proceed through the intersection and endanger the pedestrian or yield to the pedestrian and endanger the passengers? And how might an autonomous vehicle even make a decision like that?

Drones: Flying unmanned vehicles—drones—have the potential to save time and money over ground transportation. They are also being used by emergency response services to make sure that an area is safe before sending in humans to provide relief after an event like a natural disaster. There was also an explosion of interest in drones for last-mile delivery during the Covid pandemic as it removed one more potential incidence of human contact—human contact being something that many people still want to minimize post-pandemic.

However, these vehicles still require human operators—some even make the distinction between "autonomous" and "supervised autonomous" drones and vehicles. Making them fully autonomous would further save money for companies and reduce costs for consumers, but it would also make businesses more reliable as many companies struggle to fill positions.

Some of the challenges that drones face are similar to those faced by self-driving cars, and some of the potential solutions are the same. For example, even though there are fewer potential hazards in the sky than on the ground, autonomous drones need to be able to avoid crashing into other objects, including other drones, commercial and passenger aircraft, buildings, trees, and even birds.

Similar to self-driving cars, autonomous drones and other aircraft could be required to broadcast their location to avoid mid-air collisions. However, birds are less likely to comply. Further, we're not just talking about drones accidentally hitting birds—we're also talking about birds deliberately attacking drones. In 2021, drone delivery company Wing temporarily suspended operations after a series of mid-air bird attacks.[5]

In some ways, the challenges that face drones are very different from the challenges that face autonomous vehicles. For example, the marks on the road tell self-driving cars where they can go, but it is more important for drones to know where they cannot go. Certain areas are off limits to drones to preserve the security and privacy of humans and to prevent collisions with aircraft. Human pilots are able to avoid these off-limit areas, but it may be more difficult to teach autonomous drones to stay away.

Robots: Robots fall into a category similar to that of drones: they already make certain jobs easier, faster, and safer. Robots can be employed in heavy lifting, handling dangerous substances, or even in combat situations where they can explore unsafe environments and send information back to human operators. Likely the earliest situations that many of us associate with drones have to do with the exploration of sea and space—environments where humans are unable to tread. But, drones still require human operation. In their most common use cases in industry and defense, this means that the operators need to be double specialists: experts in their jobs and experts in robot operation.

Many people in the industry have even adopted the term *cobot* to describe a machine that works with a human user rather than one working independently. Many embrace the role of cobots and their ability to maintain "the human in the loop"—and indeed, there are some tasks in which the human operator provides necessary human insights—there are some monotonous or dangerous tasks human workers would rather be rid of altogether.

Depending on what a robot is tasked with, it may not need to move in the same ways as autonomous vehicles. For example, a robot working on an assembly line can remain fixed to one place as products move past. Even when robots do need to move, it can be easier for a company to design a building or campus to accommodate CV than it can be for a country to rethink a road system. Robots that constantly deal with the same task in the same environment are also less likely than self-driving cars to run into ethical dilemmas.

Robots, above all else, need to see and understand not necessarily their environment, but elements and objects within that environment. A robot may never need to find its way from Point A to Point B, but it may need to tell one bolt from another and which to tighten how far—tasks that require greater precision than the average self-driving car or autonomous drone.

Of course, we've already caught a few glimpses of what happens when robots leave the factory floor and walk among us. The mechanical engineering side of robotics still has a ways to go to say nothing of the still necessary advancements in general AI and CV in particular. For embodied AI to be useful, it needs to be able to carry out processes in the physical world, which involves a vastly different set of skills than the jobs that AI currently does for us by searching the internet. Still, the greatest achievement of Spatial Computing may be allowing us to navigate the virtual world or it may be allowing virtual agents to navigate our physical world.

Current Applications

Our look at Spatial Computing and the role of AI has already introduced a number of established and emergent industry use cases. Indeed, industries from gaming to manufacturing are already benefiting from Spatial Computing technologies like those just described as well as potentially more familiar use cases like remote co-presence.

Communication and Co-Presence

Remote collaboration is one of the earliest and most common use cases for VR. Perhaps this is because there are few industries that don't stand to benefit from it. Large companies are typically distributed over multiple campuses and even small companies increasingly work with distributed teams and with companies with distant offices.

While some meetings can still be held through 2D video conferencing, some teams prefer the sense of embodiment that comes with VR meetings and events. Depending on the software, that embodiment may be provided via virtual avatar, while at other times it is provided by volumetric capture— real-time 3D broadcasting into virtual worlds.

European finance group BNP Paribas rolled out this service on the Magic Leap One wearable Mixed Reality device in 2019, allowing clients to have remote meetings with virtually co-present representatives. The technology didn't just appear to fill an empty chair. Meetings could present virtual models of real estate locations or other 3D virtual aids shared in space between the physical and virtual meeting attendees. Because of the specialist hardware required, clients still had to go to an office to attend the meetings, but meetings with a representative whose office was in another county or country could be scheduled more quickly and conveniently—particularly when 3D virtual floor plan explorations replaced physical site visits by both parties.

Google aims to offer a similar experience through a different approach with Project Starline. Rather than a head-worn device, Project Starline uses a flat display that serves as a "magic window."[6] Specialized hardware and CV spatially capture each participant, each reconstructed on a light field display with "a sense of volume and depth" that isn't possible on a conventional screen. According to Google, this allows each participant to "talk naturally, gesture, and make eye contact" with their remote counterpart—communicating to one another rather than into a camera. Right now, Project Starline is still in the research phase and is even less accessible than Mixed Reality headsets like those used by BNP Paribas. Google anticipates making the headsets less expensive and more available.[7]

Some platforms focus strictly on bringing people into immersive virtual spaces; some distributed teams even have "offices" that only exist in virtual worlds like Virbela. The company Spatial was similarly launched as an enterprise-focused remote collaboration tool, and while it has since pivoted into the arts and culture space, it is still employed in the industry for its ease of use and customization options. Virtual models and assets can make virtual meetings the only alternative to in-person meetings.

VR and AR design are increasingly taking over from conventional ideation strategies—strategies that increasingly begin with the help of GenAI creating the first version of a model that is refined and improved by human design artists. These virtual models can be viewed collaboratively even when not all team members are present in the same physical space, saving companies the time and costs of travel expenses for distributed teams. Further, models can be viewed as life-sized or larger without the costs of physical prototypes. Products and systems designed this way often see the initial design models "re-presented" throughout the product life cycle.

For companies working with products that didn't start life as virtual models, it's not too late. Companies like Matterport offer options for creating a digital twin of an existing physical product—or a spatial map of an area for use in industrial applications, real estate, or entertainment. Where these solutions once relied on expensive 3D cameras (and still work with high-end specialized hardware), they now typically work with the camera on most modern mobile phones. Depending on the situation, companies or producers looking to work with digital assets may not even need to create their own models. Platforms like Treasury.space provide licensing and distribution services for virtual models and environments.

Just as design teams can use AR and VR for remote collaboration, production teams can call in remote support when necessary. An engineer on the floor, service worker in the field, or even emergency response personnel can choose to share their view—captured through the camera of their device—with a remote expert in the office. The remote expert can then use a touchscreen to draw notes that the technician sees in their own field of view. Or, the technician can simply video call a remote expert and watch them through a video screen in a corner of their lenses that doesn't take them away from their duties or completely occupy their attention.

Manufacturing

Many industries rely on a combination of video training modules and printed reference materials like photographs of products. Someone who works in assembly and manufacturing might start a new job by watching a video of the process, shadowing an expert, and then taking their own shift armed with photographs of what the finished product is supposed to look like.

This process is fairly safe, and it works reasonably well. However, video training modules tend to be less than captivating, shadowing an expert takes both the expert's and the trainee's time, and paper reference materials are cumbersome and can be dangerously distracting in a busy workplace. Some companies are already reimagining the whole experience with the help of Spatial Computing.

Video training modules are increasingly being replaced with AR or VR training sessions made with custom-built virtual models—exact digital replicas of parts and devices that the worker will handle on the job. While some companies have those virtual models created specifically for use in training or reference, a growing number of companies already have those virtual models handy from the design stage.

In the case of a VR training session, the immersive environment can be a digital version of the physical workplace. In the case of an AR training session, the worker can be in the actual physical environment with only some elements replaced with virtual models. A VR training experience might be interactive similar to a video game, or it might be more like a guided tour—an actual video of an expert performing a task captured through their own head-worn device and allowing the incoming engineer to step into the shoes of a seasoned technician. These don't have to be limited to training use cases—rather, a worker can step into these recorded memories any time that they need to refresh themselves on how to perform a given task.

When virtual models replace printed reference materials, the workplace becomes safer as workers are able to keep their hands free and their eyes up. AR applications mean that the wearer can continue to see the physical environment as it is because, while VR training is an improvement over video training, going back and forth between VR references isn't an improvement over juggling physical references. Image and object recognition can also automatically summon additional information like standard operating procedures and material safety data sheets. In 2019, Lockheed Martin reported the use of an AR program by Scope AR running on Microsoft HoloLens to help technicians place 57,000 cable harness fasteners in the Orion space vehicle. It turned an eight-shift job into six hours of work, resulting in a 93% reduction in cost on the project.[8]

Fewer and fewer workers are left alone with their reference materials—or even with the help of remote experts. AI is once again playing a role, helping workers navigate workflows, troubleshoot common issues, and even generate reports. With the help of CV, AI-powered programs can identify a part or piece of machinery, compare what it sees in the physical world to a digital reference model, and alert a human operator of any inconsistencies—often offering suggestions on how to correct the issue or how to proceed to the next stage in assembly.

AI is also becoming an ever-present expert by learning from each interaction above and beyond its initial knowledge base. This not only helps to record and share expert knowledge, but it also helps to codify best practices for common interactions across campuses and across time to help companies offer more uniform products and services.

Remember, too, that there is a cyclic process whereby the emerging technologies that enable advancements in manufacturing are made available through advanced manufacturing enabled by emerging technologies. Magic Leap, the Mixed Reality headset enabling some of the manufacturing processes previously described, is itself manufactured with the help of Jabil, a company that uses AI to predict supply chain trends, to optimize production schedules, and to meet the growing demand for these advanced pieces of technology.[9]

Data Visualization

AI has been a part of industry for a while now, but Spatial Computing is changing its impact. As we've discussed, companies can use AI to assess trends, make predictions, and even test for different scenarios. However, the results were usually massive datasets that would still take humans time to unpack, translate into human mediums of communication, and then properly disseminate. Thanks to AR and VR platforms that can visualize vast amounts of information in ways that make sense to even untrained humans, the kinds of insights that AI produces can have an immediate and actionable impact.

For example, BadVR offers an "immersive analytics platform" that invites users to "step inside your data." The platform not only offers data and analytics in a spatial layout, but also allows users to test different variables in real time so they aren't just looking at past statistics. They can make new decisions. One of their products, SeeSignal, allows data network service providers to visualize active service areas and dead zones in real time, allowing them to restore service more quickly after events like storms that damage infrastructure.

Human Resources

It may be assumed that human resources must certainly remain a human industry. While AI and VR aren't replacing humans in this highly personal field, these technologies are certainly proving themselves to be extremely useful tools.

Just as VR can be used to train a technician to assemble a product, it can be used to teach soft skills to management. Talespin has been developing AI-driven lessons that teach employees in management roles how to work with others, including having difficult conversations like firing people. While the company has long been using AI to create moving characters for these lessons, they have also employed AI-powered program builders that help HR teams create personalized experiences to train their teams in specific areas.

Spatial Computing doesn't only help people who already have a job. It's also helping job seekers nail that first interview. The nonprofit Dan Marino Foundation uses Spatial Computing and AI to help neurodiverse students prepare for job interviews.[10] While neurodiverse job seekers (such as people on the autism spectrum) are often mentally well-situated for high-level jobs, they often struggle with interpersonal communication, which can make it difficult for them to do well in job interviews despite an impressive skill set and work ethic. First-time job seekers with access to this kind of interview preparation have proven to have far better prospects than the national average for neurodivergent job seekers.

How did the scenarios make such a big impact? Through two main avenues. First, neurodivergent individuals often experience social anxiety, so running the simulations allowed them to prepare for real in-person interviews. Second, the headsets used collected information about each student, such as where their eyes were focused, which allowed human coaches to give them personalized suggestions like making better eye contact.

Gaming

Approximately 2.7 billion people around the world self-identify as a "gamer."[11] The gaming industry is worth more than the movie and music industry put together. Like conventional gaming, some games are played alone while others are highly social. Spatial Computing is exciting to the gaming world. AR games on mobile devices are changing the nature of play, and the growing VR games market on increasingly powerful and affordable devices makes gaming more immersive than ever.

VR games that a player enters alone will often offer them the opportunity to explore familiar worlds from an established IP like *StarWars: Tales from the Galaxy's Edge* or *Peaky Blinders: The King's Ransom*. Other VR games are built around playing and socializing with others, like the hugely popular RecRoom that was announced as a launch title on the Apple Vision Pro.

Still other games straddle the line between single-player narrative-driven games and social games that are never the same twice. Demeo, also a launch title for the Apple Vision Pro, is the Spatial Computing take on the classic tabletop role-playing game. Players can enter the virtual world alone and try their hand against the computer-played baddies or team up with friends who may be physically present or remotely co-present. Demeo is also interesting in that it offers "cross-play" between VR-enabled and 2D versions of the game, thus serving as a potential onramp for VR gamers who know the game from the more familiar desktop gaming world.

While not traditional games, brands have begun to launch virtual retail stores. Lacoste, Tommy Hilfiger, and Crate & Barrel are just a few examples of retailers that launched virtual stores in 2023. In Lacoste's virtual store, visitors were invited to find all the crocodiles (their logo) hidden in the store. For Tommy Hilfiger's retail shopping experience, Tommy Parallel Sail Club in Spatial, users were prompted to collect all the floating gems. Crate & Barrel took a slightly different approach. By interacting with products in the digital store, certain items came to life, like table settings floating off a shelf to set the table. Spatial Computing will allow brands to take their virtual stores further, adding features and personalization that apply to the customer. In her book *Reality Is Broken*, Jane McGonigal describes any good game as having "compelling goals, interesting obstacles, and well-designed feedback systems."[12] Spatial Computing in branded environments can take elements of gaming to create new shopping experiences and attract shoppers who may need to be compelled beyond normal marketing.

Spatial Computing in gaming promises many advancements for developers and players alike. Increased immersion, improved graphics, accessible gaming for differently abled people, and improved audio and social interactions are some of the features Spatial Computing in gaming has to offer.

However, it's not only the gaming industry that will be affected. Yes, developers will be able to create new types of games and push the boundaries of their imagination. But brands and businesses also have an opportunity to embrace Spatial Computing in gaming. As brands launch maps and products in online games like Roblox and Fortnite, and as they open virtual storefronts, Spatial Computing will add to those experiences, turning virtual stores into digital twins of physical landmark locations. Visitors and store workers can be motivated through gaming to shop, provide excellent customer service, or make decisions based on real-time, gamified store management. Spatial computing will push boundaries, enhance experiences, and make games fun for everyone.

Media, Sports, and Entertainment

Spatial Computing has been used in sports for so long that most people take it for granted. The placement of down and yard lines during a live broadcast of a football game was probably the first way that many of us experienced a form of AR though few of us realized its significance at the time. Of course, Spatial Computing has come a long way since then—as has its use in sports.

AR platforms like Snapchat have time and again changed the way that sports fans interact with one another. They have done so through filters that allow users to wear virtual face paint or jerseys in the colors of their favorite teams or share pictures and videos of themselves with a real-time game score on the screen. A number of sports teams have also gone all out with larger-than-life AR activations that greet fans as they arrive at the stadium or let them see those AR annotations we know from television on their phone screen as they watch the game in person.

Spatial Computing is also providing new ways to watch sports from home. Fans can watch many basketball games from virtual front-row seats through the Meta Quest, and in 2020, Apple acquired NextVR, a company that specializes in spatial sports broadcasting.[13] While we have yet to see the fruits of that action, it's safe to venture that spatial sports viewing will also be a feature of the Apple Vision Pro. In addition, the headset's launch event included the announcement of the Disney+ streaming service as being available on the headset from day one.

A number of other apps and streaming services allow VR film viewing. While some place the viewer in the middle of the event, many are more like a virtual movie theater with a screen that feels larger than life. Some even allow the viewer to watch films in a virtual theater with friends who appear as avatars in their seats.

One of the most popular use cases for the lightweight and consumer-priced Xreal Air AR glasses is screen replacement. These glasses are compatible with a wide range of consumer entertainment devices and streaming platforms. Plus, they display video games, movies, television shows, and streaming apps like YouTube on a giant virtual screen.

AR can enhance entertainment experiences in more dynamic ways as well. In 2019, HBO teamed with Magic Leap and AT&T to create "The Dead Must Die: A Magic Leap Encounter" inspired by *Game of Thrones*.[14] The experience, available in select stores, turned a physical set based on the show's King's Landing setting into a Mixed Reality battle with a virtual white walker.

Such ambitious experiences are often hosted by data network service providers because advanced connectivity is one of the emerging technologies required to host high-fidelity low-latency Mixed Reality experiences. While some of us still live in areas that are yet to be graced by 5G internet, companies like AT&T are already looking at 6G internet and beyond to allow the speeds necessary for these new kinds of data services, such as "volumetric spectrum sharing."

Challenges and Opportunities

This chapter has presented some lessons learned from the recent past, some of what enterprising companies are doing with these technologies today, and some glimpse at what the future may bring as these technologies and applications develop. The next chapter will look more closely at the convergence of Spatial Computing and AI, while future chapters will dive deeper into pioneering use cases and where these technological trends may be taking us.

Conclusions

We explored the foundations of Spatial Computing, how it works, and its current applications. We also discussed the current challenges and opportunities that are ahead. We hope that this will be a bedrock for the chapter that follows, where we will explore the symbiosis between Spatial Computing and AI.

CHAPTER 3

The Symbiosis: Spatial Computing and AI

A I and Spatial Computing are game changers, ushering in a new era where the digital and physical worlds blend seamlessly. This isn't just an upgrade or a new version of what we've had before; it's a whole new playing field.

Spatial Computing, which brings us technologies like AR and VR, lets us interact with and move through 3D spaces in ways we never thought possible. With AI, and its knack for learning, analyzing, and decision-making, we see a powerhouse combination that's opening doors to endless possibilities.

Think of AI as the brains behind the operation. It's what allows machines to make sense of and navigate complex three-dimensional spaces. Whether it's finding the best route through a busy city or designing a part for a spacecraft, AI sifts through massive amounts of spatial data to find patterns, make predictions, and offer insights that go way beyond human capabilities. This boosts the potential of Spatial Computing, making applications smarter, more intuitive, and incredibly efficient.

This isn't just tech talk—it's transforming how we live and work. In AR and VR, AI is making these experiences more interactive and lifelike, breaking down barriers between us and our digital worlds. As we talked about industries, it's a big deal in industries like healthcare, where AI-driven VR is revolutionizing how medical professionals train and prepare for the real thing. Beyond training, it's about planning and designing, too. In urban planning and architecture, AI helps professionals test and tweak their designs in virtual spaces before they ever break ground in the real world.

And let's not forget about robots. When you equip robots with AI, they're not just machines anymore—they're smart, adaptable, and capable of handling complex tasks and environments. From factories to outer space, these AI-powered robots are redefining what's possible, making tasks safer, more efficient, and a lot more interesting.

In short, the merging of AI and Spatial Computing is a big leap forward. It's not just about making things better; it's about opening up a world of new possibilities, solving tough problems, and exploring uncharted territory. As we step into this new era, the fusion of these technologies promises to reshape our world in ways we're just beginning to imagine.

Overview of AI-Driven Spatial Applications

AI has become a cornerstone in shaping Spatial Computing applications. This integration of AI with spatial technologies like AR and VR is not just an enhancement of existing capabilities, but also a transformative shift that is redefining how we interact with our environment and virtual spaces. These AI-driven spatial applications are revolutionizing various sectors, from navigation and training to design and agriculture, demonstrating the versatility and depth of this technology.

Navigating the world with AR: One of the most direct impacts of this integration is seen in AR navigation and wayfinding apps. These applications use AI to provide real-time, intuitive navigation guidance in AR. This technology is especially useful in unfamiliar environments, helping users find their way with ease. By overlaying digital information onto the real world, these apps make navigation more interactive and informative, enhancing the user experience (UX) significantly.

Training in virtual worlds: In the realm of training and education, AI-powered VR simulations are game-changers. Fields like healthcare, aviation, and the military are already reaping the benefits of this technology. Trainees can practice and hone their skills in realistic, risk-free virtual environments, preparing them for real-world scenarios. This application of AI in VR provides a safe yet highly effective training ground, revolutionizing traditional training methodologies.

Interacting with the world through AI: AI's role in enhancing AR experiences extends to object recognition as well. AR applications now use AI to recognize and interact with real-world objects. Whether it's scanning QR codes, translating text in real time, or providing detailed information about products through image recognition, AI is making AR more interactive and useful in everyday life.

Making sense of space with AI: Spatial data analytics represents another crucial area where AI is making a significant impact. By analyzing spatial data, AI helps in making informed decisions in urban planning, resource management, and disaster response. This application is particularly important for businesses and governments in planning and executing strategies that are spatially optimized and data driven.

Revolutionizing design and retail: In industrial and interior design, AI-driven applications are transforming how spaces are planned and visualized. From optimizing factory layouts for efficiency to helping users visualize and personalize their living spaces in virtual showrooms, AI is playing a key role in making design more accessible and customized.

Enhancing healthcare and gaming: AI-driven spatial applications are also making strides in healthcare, with VR environments being used for surgical simulations and patient diagnosis. In the gaming industry, AI is used to create more dynamic and responsive environments, making the gaming experience more immersive and interactive.

Agricultural and urban planning advancements: In agriculture, AI's application to spatial data is improving crop management and optimizing farming processes. Similarly, in urban planning, AI models simulate various spatial configurations, aiding in the development and planning of cities.

Collaborating in virtual spaces: The combination of Spatial Computing and AI is revolutionizing how we collaborate remotely. By enabling participants to interact in shared virtual spaces, these technologies are enhancing teamwork and communication, breaking down the barriers of distance and physical limitations.

In summary, the integration of AI with Spatial Computing technologies is creating a multitude of applications that are transforming how we perceive, interact with, and manipulate both physical and virtual environments. This symbiosis is not only enhancing UXs, but also solving complex problems across various sectors, signaling a new era of technological innovation and application.

Robotics is such a big area for the combination of AI and Spatial Computing that we've devoted a whole section to it next.

Robotics

The integration of AI into the field of robotics marks a significant evolution in our technological capabilities, opening new frontiers in efficiency, precision, and automation. This fusion has given rise to a diverse array of AI-driven robots, each tailored to specific tasks and environments, reshaping how tasks are performed across various industries. From the inner workings of warehouses to the vastness of outer space, the application of AI in robotics is not just enhancing existing processes, but also enabling new possibilities that were once beyond our reach.

Autonomous Robots in Warehouses

Functionality: AI-powered robots in warehouses are designed to automate tasks like picking, packing, sorting, and transporting goods. These robots use sensors, machine vision, and AI algorithms to navigate the warehouse floor, avoiding obstacles and optimizing routes.

Impact: By automating repetitive and physically demanding tasks, these robots enhance operational efficiency, reduce errors, and cut down on the time it takes to move items around. This leads to faster order fulfillment and a more efficient supply chain.

Technological advances: Advanced ML models enable these robots to continuously improve their performance based on real-time data. Integration with warehouse management systems ensures synchronization with inventory levels and order processing.

Robotic Surgical Assistants

Functionality: In healthcare, robotic surgical assistants are equipped with AI to provide surgeons with enhanced precision and control during operations. These systems often feature robotic arms controlled by surgeons, offering greater dexterity and stability than the human hand.

Impact: The use of AI in robotic surgery helps in minimizing incisions, reducing patient recovery time, and decreasing the risk of complications. By enhancing spatial awareness, these robots allow for more accurate and less invasive surgeries.

Technological advances: AI algorithms can assist in planning surgical procedures by analyzing patient data and medical images. Real-time feedback and ML can help surgeons make more informed decisions during operations.

Agricultural Robots

Functionality: AI-driven agricultural robots are used for tasks like planting, weeding, harvesting, and monitoring crop health. They utilize sensors and AI to assess soil conditions, plant health, and optimal harvesting times.

Impact: These robots improve the efficiency of farming operations, reduce the need for manual labor, and minimize the use of resources like water and fertilizers. This leads to higher crop yields and more sustainable farming practices.

Technological advances: ML models enable these robots to adapt to different crop types and environmental conditions. Drones and robotic ground vehicles work together to provide comprehensive data on crop health and growth patterns.

Delivery Robots

Functionality: Autonomous delivery robots use AI to navigate through urban environments to deliver packages. These robots are typically equipped with cameras, GPS, and sensors to identify the best routes and avoid obstacles.

Impact: Delivery robots offer a solution to the "last mile" delivery problem, reducing delivery times and costs. They are particularly useful in dense urban areas where traditional delivery vehicles face challenges.

Technological advances: Advanced navigation algorithms and real-time data processing allow these robots to operate safely in busy urban environments. Integration with online retail platforms ensures efficient dispatch and tracking of deliveries.

Robotic Mapping and Exploration

Functionality: AI-equipped robots used for mapping and exploration can venture into uncharted or hazardous areas, such as deep sea environments or other planets. They collect data, take samples, and provide detailed maps of these areas.

Impact: These robots enable the exploration of environments that are inaccessible or too dangerous for humans, expanding our understanding of the world and beyond. They are crucial in scientific research, resource discovery, and environmental monitoring.

Technological advances: Robotics in this field often use AI for autonomous decision-making, allowing them to adapt to unexpected situations. ML algorithms help in processing and interpreting the vast amounts of data collected during exploration missions.

Robotic Manufacturing and Assembly

Functionality: In manufacturing, AI-driven robots perform tasks like assembly, welding, and painting. They are programmed to work alongside humans, often in collaborative settings, to carry out precise and repetitive tasks.

Impact: The use of these robots leads to increased production efficiency, improved product quality, and enhanced worker safety. They are adaptable to different tasks, making manufacturing processes more flexible.

Technological advances: Machine vision systems and tactile sensors allow these robots to handle delicate components and adapt to varying assembly conditions. AI algorithms enable them to learn from their environment and improve task execution over time.

Robotic Assistants for Elderly and Disabled

Functionality: These AI-powered robots assist with daily tasks, provide companionship, and enhance mobility for the elderly and individuals with disabilities. They can perform tasks like fetching items, providing medication reminders, and offering support for physical movement.

Impact: These robotic assistants improve the quality of life for their users by providing help with daily activities and reducing the need for constant human caregiving. This can lead to increased independence and well-being for the elderly and disabled.

Technological advances: AI enables these robots to understand and respond to voice commands, recognize objects, and learn individual preferences and routines. They can also monitor health parameters and alert caregivers in case of emergencies.

Robotic Vehicles and Drones

Functionality: Autonomous vehicles and drones utilize AI for spatial navigation, a crucial aspect in applications, such as transportation, surveillance, and delivery. These systems are equipped with sensors, cameras, and GPS, allowing them to understand and navigate their environment.

Impact: In transportation, autonomous vehicles are set to revolutionize how we travel, reducing accidents and improving traffic flow. Drones, on the other hand, are being used for a range of purposes, including aerial surveillance, agricultural monitoring, and rapid delivery of goods.

Technological advances: ML algorithms enable these vehicles and drones to make real-time decisions based on environmental data, improving safety and efficiency. Continuous advancements in sensor technology and data processing are enhancing their capabilities and reliability.

Construction and Demolition Robots

Functionality: In the construction industry, AI-driven robots perform tasks like bricklaying, welding, and demolition. These robots are designed to handle heavy materials and operate in challenging environments.

Impact: The use of robots in construction and demolition enhances safety by reducing human exposure to hazardous tasks. It also improves efficiency, as robots can work continuously and with precision, speeding up construction timelines.

Technological advances: These robots often use AI to plan and execute tasks, adapting to different construction scenarios. They can work autonomously or in coordination with human workers, offering flexibility in various construction processes.

Search and Rescue Robots

Functionality: In disaster scenarios, search and rescue robots equipped with AI are deployed to navigate through rubble and hazardous environments. They are designed to locate and assist survivors where human rescuers might not be able to reach.

Impact: These robots are invaluable in emergency situations, able to quickly search large areas and provide real-time data to rescue teams. They can operate in environments affected by natural disasters, fires, or structural collapses, potentially saving lives and improving response times.

Technological advances: Equipped with thermal imaging, audio detection, and other sensors, these robots can identify signs of life and navigate through debris. ML algorithms help them to improve their search patterns and decision-making in complex environments.

AI in Robotic Toys and Companions

Functionality: AI enhances robotic toys and companions, making them interactive and capable of learning. These robots can recognize faces, respond to voice commands, and adapt to user preferences.

Impact: Robotic toys and companions offer entertainment and educational value, especially for children. They can assist in learning languages, math, and other skills through interactive play. For adults, they provide companionship and can even assist with daily reminders and tasks.

Technological advances: Advances in natural language processing and machine vision allow these robots to interact in more human-like ways, understanding and responding to verbal and visual cues.

Robotics in Space Exploration

Functionality: AI-powered robots in space exploration are designed to operate in extreme environments, conducting experiments, collecting data, and even performing repairs on spacecraft and satellites.

Impact: These robots extend our reach into space, enabling the exploration of planets, moons, and asteroids. They provide critical data that helps us understand our universe and the potential for life beyond Earth.

Technological advances: Space exploration robots use AI for autonomous navigation and decision-making, particularly important in environments where real-time communication with Earth is not possible.

Autonomous Cleaning Robots

Functionality: AI-equipped cleaning robots are designed to autonomously navigate indoor spaces like offices and homes, cleaning floors and surfaces. They use sensors to map out areas and avoid obstacles.

Impact: These robots offer convenience and efficiency in maintaining cleanliness, especially in large facilities like hospitals, offices, and hotels. They can operate autonomously, freeing up human resources for other tasks.

Technological advances: Continuous improvements in sensor technology and AI algorithms have enhanced the efficiency and effectiveness of these cleaning robots, allowing them to cover more area and handle different types of surfaces.

AI-Enhanced Robotic Exoskeletons

Functionality: Robotic exoskeletons with AI support are wearable devices that assist individuals with mobility impairments. These systems use sensors and AI to adjust to the user's movements and provide assistance as needed.

Impact: These exoskeletons enhance the mobility and independence of individuals with disabilities or those recovering from injuries. They can be used for rehabilitation and to assist with daily tasks, improving the quality of life for users.

Technological advances: Advances in sensor technology and AI allow these exoskeletons to adapt to various levels of mobility and provide personalized support. This improves the user's comfort and the effectiveness of the assistance provided.

Educational Robots

Functionality: AI-driven educational robots are used to engage students in learning activities. These robots can teach various subjects, respond to questions, and even assess student progress.

Impact: These robots make learning more interactive and engaging, especially for subjects like science, technology, engineering, and mathematics (STEM). They can provide personalized learning experiences and foster problem-solving and critical-thinking skills.

Technological advances: AI enables these robots to adapt to different learning styles and levels. They can assess student responses and tailor their teaching methods accordingly, making education more accessible and effective.

Robotic Inspection and Maintenance

Functionality: AI-powered robots designed for inspection and maintenance are tasked with monitoring and upkeep of critical infrastructure, such as pipelines, bridges, power lines, and industrial equipment. Equipped with sensors, cameras, and sometimes even drones, these robots can access and assess areas that are difficult, dangerous, or impossible for humans to reach.

Impact: The application of these robots significantly enhances the safety and efficiency of infrastructure maintenance. By enabling early detection of potential issues and performing routine maintenance, they help prevent accidents and costly downtime. These robots are crucial in industries where infrastructure failure can have severe consequences, like oil and gas, energy, and transportation.

Technological advances: Advancements in machine vision, sensor technology, and AI algorithms allow these robots to detect anomalies, cracks, corrosion, and other signs of wear and tear accurately. Some are equipped with robotic arms for performing repairs in situ, while others use drones for aerial inspections.

Hospitality and Service Robots

Functionality: In the hospitality industry, AI-driven robots are employed for various services, including room delivery, food service, and guest assistance. These robots can navigate through hotels and restaurants, interacting with guests to provide services or information.

Impact: The use of robots in hospitality settings enhances customer service by providing quick and efficient responses to guest needs. They can handle repetitive tasks, allowing human staff to focus on more complex customer service aspects, thereby improving overall operational efficiency.

Technological advances: These robots often integrate AI with natural language processing to interact with guests in multiple languages. Their navigation systems are sophisticated enough to maneuver in crowded and dynamic environments like hotel lobbies or restaurant floors.

Security Robots

Functionality: AI-enhanced security robots are designed to patrol and monitor large areas, such as warehouses, corporate campuses, and public spaces. They use a combination of cameras, sensors, and sometimes facial recognition technology to detect unauthorized activities or potential security threats.

Impact: These robots augment traditional security measures by providing continuous surveillance, especially in areas that are challenging or risky for human guards. They can quickly alert human operators to potential threats, improving response times and overall security.

Technological advances: Advanced ML algorithms enable these robots to distinguish between normal and suspicious activities. Some are equipped with thermal imaging for night patrols, and others can integrate data from various sources, like security cameras and alarms, for comprehensive monitoring.

Retail Robots

Functionality: In the retail sector, autonomous robots assist in tasks like customer wayfinding, inventory management, and providing product recommendations. These robots can navigate store aisles, interact with customers, and perform stock checks.

Impact: Retail robots enhance the shopping experience by providing customers with information and assistance, leading to increased customer satisfaction. For retailers, these robots offer efficient inventory management, ensuring shelves are stocked and reducing the likelihood of stockouts.

Technological advances: These robots use machine vision to identify products and assess inventory levels. Some are equipped with interactive screens for customer interaction, and their AI algorithms can provide personalized recommendations based on customer queries and buying patterns.

The deployment of AI-driven robots across these varied industries showcases the versatility and potential of robotic applications. Whether it's maintaining critical infrastructure, enhancing customer service, bolstering security, or improving retail experiences, these robots are not only optimizing processes, but also opening new avenues for innovation and customer engagement. By combining advanced AI with sophisticated robotic systems, these applications are setting new standards for efficiency, safety, and service quality across multiple sectors.

How AI Improves UXs

The advent of AI in Spatial Computing has ushered in a new era of UXs, one where the interaction between humans and digital environments is more intuitive, immersive, and personalized than ever before. AI acts as the cornerstone of these advancements, significantly enhancing the capabilities of AR and VR applications. And as we've been saying, its influence extends across a wide spectrum of industries, transforming the way we interact with, perceive, and utilize digital content. The integration of AI in Spatial Computing not only makes these experiences more engaging, but also tailors them to individual user needs and preferences, thereby broadening their applicability and impact.

One of the most noticeable improvements brought about by AI in AR and VR is the enhancement of realistic object interactions. Through sophisticated AI algorithms, virtual objects within these environments can be manipulated and interacted with in a manner that closely mimics real-world interactions. This advancement significantly boosts the immersion factor, allowing users to feel a deeper connection with the virtual environment. Additionally, AI-powered natural language (NLP) understanding and speech recognition technologies are making strides in making communication with AR and VR environments more natural and intuitive. Users can now interact with virtual entities using voice commands, facilitating a more fluid and human-like interaction. The incorporation of gesture recognition technology further adds to this intuitive experience, allowing users to navigate and control their virtual environment through natural hand movements and gestures.

The role of AI in Spatial Computing extends beyond just improving user interaction; it also enhances the overall quality and relevance of the UX experience. AI-driven spatial mapping and awareness enable AR and VR systems to have a more profound understanding of the physical environment, thus allowing for more accurate placement of virtual objects and enhancing the realism of Mixed Reality experiences. Personalization is another key aspect where AI makes a significant impact. By analyzing user preferences and behaviors, AI can tailor AR and VR content to individual users, making experiences more engaging and pertinent. From dynamic environments that adjust in real time to user actions in gaming to AI-driven narratives in storytelling and realistic healthcare simulations, AI is reshaping the landscape of UXs in Spatial Computing. This comprehensive integration of AI not only enhances the aesthetic appeal of these experiences through improved visuals and sound, but also ensures inclusivity by providing accessibility features for users with disabilities. In essence, AI is the driving force behind making AR and VR experiences more human-centric, accessible, and resonant with the real world.

Here is more detail on specific aspects:

Storytelling: In AR and VR, AI-driven storytelling takes UXs to a new level. Through adaptive narratives and characters, stories can unfold based on user decisions and actions, creating a unique and personalized journey for each user. These AI systems use complex algorithms to analyze user choices, adapting the storyline in real time. This approach allows for multiple story branches, where each decision made by the user can lead to different outcomes, akin to a choose-your-own-adventure book but in a digital, interactive format. This technology is particularly powerful in educational and entertainment applications, where engaging storytelling is crucial.

Healthcare simulations: AI in healthcare simulations offers unprecedented realism and interactivity. By simulating patient behaviors and responses, AI provides healthcare professionals with realistic scenarios for practice. This includes replicating a wide range of medical conditions and patient reactions to treatments, allowing for diverse training experiences. These simulations are critical for preparing medical professionals for real-life situations, helping them develop diagnostic skills, bedside manners, and surgical techniques in a risk-free environment.

Eye and gaze tracking: Eye and gaze tracking technology in VR, powered by AI, enhances user interaction by allowing control through eye movements. This technology tracks where the user is looking and adjusts the VR environment accordingly, enabling hands-free navigation and interaction. This feature is particularly beneficial in scenarios where manual interaction is limited or impractical, such as in accessibility applications or complex training simulations. It also adds a layer of immersion, as the environment responds to the most natural and intuitive of human actions—looking.

Emotion recognition: Emotion recognition in AR and VR, driven by AI, adds an empathetic dimension to these technologies. By detecting and analyzing users' facial expressions, voice tones, and physiological responses, AI can tailor the experience to match their emotional state. This technology can be used to adjust the difficulty of a game when a player is frustrated or to change the storyline based on the user's emotional responses, making experiences more empathetic and engaging.

Enhanced and generated visuals: AI-driven image processing and upscaling in AR and VR significantly enhance the visual quality of these experiences. By using techniques like ML and GenAI, these systems can produce high-resolution, lifelike graphics, even from lower-quality inputs. This enhancement is crucial for creating immersive and visually appealing environments, especially in applications where realism is key, such as in virtual tourism or real estate showcases.

Noise cancellation: AI-enhanced noise cancellation in VR improves the audio experience by filtering out background noise and enhancing spatial audio. This technology is essential in creating a fully immersive environment, as clear and directional sound is as important as visual fidelity. Whether in gaming, training simulations, or virtual meetings, effective noise cancellation ensures that users can focus on the VR experience without external distractions.

Accessibility: AI-driven accessibility features in AR and VR make these technologies more inclusive. By offering alternative input methods, such as voice commands or eye tracking, along with audio descriptions and other accommodations, AR and VR become accessible to users with various disabilities. This inclusivity is crucial in extending the benefits of AR and VR to a wider audience, ensuring that everyone can experience the wonders of these technologies.

Simulated training environments: AI creates highly realistic and adaptable training environments across industries. In sectors like aviation and manufacturing, these simulations provide a safe and controlled setting for users to practice and hone their skills. The AI algorithms can simulate real-world scenarios, machinery behavior, and even emergency situations, offering a comprehensive training experience that closely mirrors actual working conditions.

Dynamic object behavior: AI enables dynamic and intelligent behavior in objects and characters within VR environments. This capability means that virtual entities can act and react in a context-aware manner, adapting to user interactions and environmental changes. In gaming and simulations, this leads to more realistic and engaging scenarios as the virtual world responds in a lifelike and believable way to user actions.

In conclusion, AI has revolutionized the domain of Spatial Computing, particularly in AR and VR technologies, by enhancing the depth, realism, and personalization of UXs. The integration of AI in these realms has not only made interactions with digital environments more intuitive and engaging, but has also opened up new possibilities for personalized and adaptive experiences. From creating immersive and interactive storytelling to providing highly realistic training simulations in healthcare, AI has proven to be a transformative force. It has made significant strides in making user interfaces more natural through eye and gaze tracking, and in responding empathetically to user emotions. Furthermore, AI has substantially improved the visual and auditory quality of AR and VR experiences, making them more lifelike and immersive.

The incorporation of AI into Spatial Computing has also addressed broader needs like accessibility, ensuring that these advanced technologies are inclusive and available to a wider range of users. The dynamic adaptation of virtual environments to user actions and the intelligent behavior of objects and characters within these environments are testaments to the evolving capabilities of AI in this field.

Overall, AI has not only enhanced the UX in AR and VR, but it has also significantly expanded the potential applications of these technologies across various industries, making them more versatile, efficient, and accessible. This integration marks a significant leap forward in how we interact with and benefit from digital environments, paving the way for even more innovative and immersive experiences in the future.

Business Benefits and Other Human Benefits

The convergence of AI and Spatial Computing is revolutionizing both the business world and various aspects of human life. This powerful combination is not only reshaping how businesses operate, but also enhancing human experiences in numerous ways. From improving operational efficiency to offering immersive entertainment, the synergy between AI and Spatial Computing is paving the way for a future where technology seamlessly integrates with daily activities.

In the business sector, AI and Spatial Computing are instrumental in driving improved efficiency, enhanced decision-making, and cost reduction. AI's ability to process and analyze vast amounts of data complements the immersive and interactive capabilities of Spatial Computing, leading to more informed decisions and efficient operations. Personalized customer experiences, powered by AI, are transforming the retail and service industries, offering new ways to engage and satisfy customers. Furthermore, the competitive advantage gained through these technologies is helping businesses stay ahead in a rapidly evolving market.

Beyond the realm of business, the human benefits of AI and Spatial Computing are equally significant. In healthcare, AI-assisted diagnostics and treatments, combined with AR and VR applications, are improving patient care and outcomes. Education and training are being redefined through AI-enhanced learning experiences and interactive Spatial Computing applications, making education more engaging and effective. The entertainment and gaming industries are experiencing a renaissance with immersive and interactive experiences that were once the stuff of science fiction. Additionally, these technologies are playing a crucial role in promoting accessibility and inclusivity, providing assistive solutions for people with disabilities, and contributing to environmental sustainability through optimized resource management.

As we explore the multifaceted impacts of AI and Spatial Computing, it becomes clear that these technologies are not just tools for business innovation, but also catalysts for improving the quality of human life. They are redefining what is possible, transforming challenges into opportunities and opening up new horizons in virtually every sector.

Revolutionizing Business through AI and Spatial Computing

In a temporary business landscape, the integration of AI and Spatial Computing has emerged as a transformative force. These technologies are not merely augmenting existing processes, but are also reshaping them, driving unparalleled efficiency, enhancing decision-making, reducing costs, personalizing customer experiences, and providing a competitive advantage.

Improved efficiency and productivity: AI's role in enhancing operational efficiency is monumental. By automating routine tasks, AI systems free up human resources for more complex and creative work. For instance, AI algorithms can analyze large data sets faster and more accurately than humans, identifying patterns and anomalies that might go unnoticed. This capability is crucial in areas like fraud detection in banking or demand forecasting in retail.

Spatial Computing further complements this by optimizing workflows. In manufacturing, for instance, Spatial Computing tools can design factory layouts that maximize efficiency, simulate assembly line processes, and even guide robots and workers in real time, reducing errors and increasing productivity. A notable example is Amazon's use of AI and robotics in its warehouses, where AI algorithms predict order trends and robots assist in sorting and transporting goods, significantly speeding up the order fulfillment process.

Enhanced decision-making: AI-driven data analysis offers businesses deep insights, aiding in more informed decision-making. AI systems can sift through vast amounts of data to provide actionable insights, predict market trends, and identify customer preferences. This capability allows businesses to make decisions based on data-driven insights rather than intuition.

Spatial Computing aids in visualizing complex data in an understandable format. For example, in real estate, Spatial Computing can visualize market trends and property data in a 3D space, helping investors and developers to make better-informed decisions about where to build or invest. A case study illustrating this is how JPMorgan Chase uses AI to analyze legal documents and extract critical data points, reducing review time by more than 360,000 hours annually.

Cost reduction: AI significantly contributes to cost reduction by streamlining operations and enhancing efficiency. In supply chain management, AI algorithms predict demand and optimize inventory levels, reducing wastage and storage costs. AI-driven predictive maintenance in manufacturing can forecast equipment failures before they occur, preventing costly downtimes.

Spatial Computing also plays a key role in remote operations. In industries, such as mining and oil exploration, Spatial Computing allows for remote monitoring of sites, reducing the need for physical presence, which in turn, cuts travel and staffing costs. An example is BP's deployment of AI and Spatial Computing for remote monitoring of oil rigs, leading to a significant reduction in operational costs.

Personalized customer experiences: AI has revolutionized customer experience by enabling personalization at scale. AI-driven recommendation systems, like those used by Netflix and Amazon, analyze user preferences to suggest products or content, enhancing user engagement and satisfaction.

In retail, Spatial Computing creates immersive shopping experiences. Virtual try-ons and interactive 3D models in online shopping are becoming increasingly popular, thanks to Spatial Computing technologies. A success story in this realm is IKEA's AR app, which lets customers visualize furniture in their homes before purchasing, significantly enhancing customer satisfaction and reducing return rates.

Competitive advantage: Last, AI and Spatial Computing confer a competitive edge to businesses. They enable companies to innovate faster, respond to market changes more agilely, and offer unique customer experiences. Companies like Tesla integrate AI and Spatial Computing in their vehicles for autonomous driving features, setting them apart from traditional automakers.

The future prospects for competition in businesses leveraging AI and Spatial Computing are vast. As these technologies advance, they will continue to provide companies with new ways to outperform their rivals, whether through improved customer understanding, more efficient operations, or innovative products and services.

Other Human Benefits of AI and Spatial Computing

Spatial Computing and AI are at the forefront of technological innovation, significantly impacting various aspects of daily life. These technologies are not only advancing industries, but also enhancing human experiences in numerous fields such as healthcare, education, entertainment, accessibility, and environmental sustainability. By harnessing the power of AI's data processing capabilities and the immersive nature of Spatial Computing, we are witnessing a transformative era where technology is not just a tool, but a partner in driving progress and creating more inclusive, efficient, and sustainable solutions. In this section, we focus on the diverse and far-reaching benefits of AI and Spatial Computing, showcasing their pivotal role in shaping a better future.

Improved Healthcare

The healthcare sector is undergoing a transformative change due to AI and Spatial Computing, resulting in enhanced patient care and outcomes.

AI-assisted diagnostics and treatment: AI algorithms are revolutionizing diagnostics by analyzing medical images with higher precision and speed than human practitioners. For example, AI systems can detect anomalies in X-rays and MRIs, identifying diseases like cancer at early stages, thereby increasing the chances of successful treatment. In treatment, AI models are used to predict patient responses to different therapies, enabling personalized medicine approaches.

AI-assisted surgery utilizing AR and VR: AR and VR are proving instrumental in surgical procedures. Surgeons use AR to superimpose a digital overlay on the patient's body during surgery, providing real-time, 3D anatomical information, which enhances precision and reduces risks. VR simulations are used for surgical training, allowing surgeons to practice complex procedures in a virtual environment, improving their skills without risking patient safety.

Spatial Computing in telemedicine: Spatial Computing technologies are expanding the reach of healthcare through telemedicine. Patients in remote or underserved areas can receive consultations and diagnoses via telemedicine platforms, which use Spatial Computing to offer more interactive and comprehensive medical consultations. This technology is particularly beneficial for monitoring chronic conditions and providing mental health services.

Patient outcomes and healthcare accessibility: The integration of AI and Spatial Computing in healthcare leads to improved patient outcomes. Faster and more accurate diagnoses, personalized treatment plans, and minimally invasive surgery are some of the direct benefits. Additionally, these technologies make healthcare more accessible, reducing geographical barriers and enabling continuous patient monitoring.

Education and Training
AI and Spatial Computing are reshaping the educational landscape by enhancing learning experiences and skill development.

AI-enhanced learning experiences: AI personalizes learning by adapting educational content to the learner's style and pace. AI systems can assess a student's understanding of a topic and provide customized resources or exercises. This personalized approach helps in addressing individual learning gaps and enhances the overall educational experience.

Spatial Computing in interactive education: Spatial Computing, through AR and VR, brings an immersive dimension to education. Students can explore virtual laboratories, historical sites, or even the human body in 3D, making learning more engaging and effective. For instance, medical students can practice anatomy using VR models, providing a hands-on learning experience without the need for physical dissection.

Skill development and knowledge transfer: Spatial Computing tools also facilitate skill development in vocational training. For example, VR simulations are used to train mechanics, electricians, and pilots, allowing them to practice in safe, controlled environments. This hands-on experience enhances skill acquisition and prepares learners for real-world scenarios.

Enhanced Entertainment and Gaming

The entertainment and gaming industries are among the most visibly transformed by AI and Spatial Computing.

Immersive gaming experiences: AI and Spatial Computing create deeply immersive gaming experiences. AI algorithms can generate dynamic game worlds that respond to player actions, creating a unique experience for each player. VR and AR bring games to life, allowing players to immerse themselves in 3D worlds, enhancing the sense of presence and engagement.

Spatial Computing's impact on entertainment: Beyond gaming, Spatial Computing is transforming other entertainment forms, like cinema and live events. AR applications provide interactive experiences in museums and theme parks, while VR allows users to experience concerts or travel destinations virtually.

Recreational benefits for users: These technologies offer significant recreational benefits, providing new forms of entertainment that are more interactive and engaging. They also offer accessible leisure activities for individuals who may be physically unable to participate in traditional forms of recreation.

Accessibility and Inclusivity

AI and Spatial Computing are instrumental in making technology more accessible and inclusive.

Empowering people with disabilities: AI and Spatial Computing technologies provide assistive solutions that enhance the independence of individuals with disabilities. For example, AI-driven voice assistants and eye-tracking software enable people with mobility impairments to interact with technology. AR can overlay sign language interpreters on screens for the deaf, and VR can simulate environments for training and rehabilitation.

Assistive technologies and inclusive design: These technologies encourage inclusive design in software and hardware development. AI algorithms can adapt interfaces to suit individual needs, and Spatial Computing can create virtual environments tailored for accessibility training and awareness.

Success stories of improved accessibility: There are numerous success stories where AI and Spatial Computing have improved accessibility. Microsoft's Seeing AI app, which describes the world for the visually impaired, and Google's Project Euphonia, which helps people with speech impairments communicate, are notable examples.

Environmental Benefits

AI and Spatial Computing also play a crucial role in environmental sustainability.

AI-driven resource optimization: AI optimizes the use of resources in industries like energy and agriculture. For instance, AI algorithms forecast energy demand, enabling smarter grid management and reducing waste. In agriculture, AI predicts crop yields and optimizes irrigation and fertilization, conserving resources and increasing efficiency.

Spatial Computing for sustainable practices: Spatial Computing aids in visualizing and planning sustainable practices. For example, VR can simulate environmental impacts of construction projects, helping planners make more eco-friendly decisions. AR applications can educate the public about environmental issues in an engaging manner.

Reduction of environmental impact: By optimizing resource use and aiding in sustainable planning, AI and Spatial Computing contribute to reducing the environmental footprint of human activities. These technologies provide tools for monitoring and mitigating climate change impacts, representing a significant step toward a more sustainable future.

In conclusion, AI and Spatial Computing are not just technological advancements; they represent a paradigm shift in how we approach healthcare, education, entertainment, accessibility, and environmental sustainability. Their far-reaching implications extend beyond mere convenience, offering profound benefits that enhance human life and the environment.

Future Trends in AI and Spatial Computing

The integration of AI and Spatial Computing is not just reshaping current technologies, but also paving the way for groundbreaking future trends. These developments promise to significantly expand the capabilities and applications of AI-powered AR and VR, influencing various aspects of our lives. Let's explore these trends in more detail.

Predictions for Everyday Life

In the near future, AI and Spatial Computing will seamlessly blend into our daily lives, transforming homes, workplaces, and public spaces into more responsive and interactive environments. Advancements in human–machine interfaces, like brain-computer interfaces (BCIs), AR and VR will revolutionize how we interact with technology.

Seamless integration into everyday life: In the future, we can expect AI and Spatial Computing to become more seamlessly integrated into our everyday lives. This integration will go beyond smartphones and computers to include everyday objects and environments. Homes, workplaces, and public spaces will become more interactive and responsive, with AI-driven Spatial Computing technologies embedded in the fabric of these environments.

Advanced human–machine interfaces: The evolution of interfaces that allow for more natural human–machine interaction is imminent. Future interfaces will likely rely on BCIs, where users can control AR and VR environments through thought alone. This technology will revolutionize how we interact with digital content, making the experience more intuitive and accessible.

Ubiquitous AR and VR: AR and VR will become more prevalent in various sectors, including education, healthcare, entertainment, and retail. We'll see an increase in AR for everyday tasks like navigation, shopping, and social interactions, while VR will become more common for remote work, virtual travel, and immersive learning.

Advancements in AI Algorithms for Spatial Awareness

The future of AI algorithms is set to significantly enhance spatial awareness in AR and VR technologies. These advancements will enable the creation of highly accurate and detailed 3D maps of the world in real time, greatly enhancing the realism and interactivity of AR and VR experiences.

Enhanced real-world mapping: Future AI algorithms will offer more sophisticated spatial awareness and mapping capabilities. These advancements will enable AR and VR devices to construct highly accurate and detailed 3D maps of the world in real time, enhancing the realism and interactivity of AR and VR experiences.

Predictive and contextual awareness: AI systems will become more adept at understanding and predicting user behavior and environmental context. This development will lead to more personalized and contextually relevant AR and VR experiences, where the content dynamically adapts not just to user actions, but also to their anticipated needs and preferences.

Real-time environmental interaction: We can anticipate advancements in AI that enable real-time interaction with changing environments. For example, AR systems could be used to overlay information on a construction site, showing changes in real time as work progresses, or in emergency scenarios, providing critical information to responders onsite.

Expanding the Scope of AI-Powered AR and VR

AI-powered AR and VR are poised to revolutionize sectors like education, healthcare, social interaction, urban planning, entertainment, and environmental sustainability. They will provide immersive learning experiences, enhance healthcare with advanced diagnostics and remote surgeries, and transform social and collaborative experiences in virtual spaces. In urban development, they'll contribute to smarter city planning and infrastructure management. The entertainment industry will see more personalized content, while ethical and privacy concerns will become increasingly important.

Enhanced learning and skill development: Future trends in AI-powered AR and VR will heavily impact education and skill training. These technologies will offer more immersive and interactive learning experiences, simulating real-world scenarios for a wide range of professions, from medical to mechanical, in a safe and controlled environment.

Healthcare innovation: In healthcare, the future of AI and Spatial Computing looks particularly promising. We can expect more advanced diagnostic tools, personalized treatment plans based on patient data analysis, and even remote surgeries performed through AR and VR platforms.

Social and collaborative experiences: Social interactions and collaborative work will be transformed by AI-enhanced AR and VR. These technologies will create virtual spaces where people can interact and collaborate as if they were physically present together, breaking down geographical barriers and fostering a more connected world.

Smart cities and infrastructure: AI and Spatial Computing will play a significant role in the development of smart cities. These technologies can be used for urban planning, traffic management, and enhancing public services through more efficient and responsive systems.

Personalized entertainment and media: In the entertainment sector, we'll see more personalized and interactive content, driven by AI. Movies, games, and other media will adapt to user preferences and responses, creating unique experiences for each viewer or player.

Ethical and privacy considerations: As AI and Spatial Computing become more prevalent, ethical and privacy issues will become increasingly important. The development of these technologies will need to be balanced with considerations around data privacy, security, and the ethical implications of AI decisions.

Environmental sustainability: Finally, AI and Spatial Computing will contribute significantly to environmental sustainability. These technologies will help in efficient resource management, monitoring environmental changes, and developing sustainable practices.

In summary, the future of AI and Spatial Computing holds immense potential, promising to transform how we interact with our world and each other. These advancements will bring about new opportunities and challenges, reshaping various industries and aspects of daily life. As these technologies evolve, they will offer more immersive, personalized, and efficient experiences, heralding a new era of human–computer interaction.

Conclusions

As we reflect on the expansive journey through the symbiotic relationship between AI and Spatial Computing, it's evident that this alliance is not just transformative, but also foundational to the future of technological advancement. The interplay between AI's analytical prowess and Spatial Computing's ability to integrate digital information into our physical world has set the stage for a multitude of groundbreaking applications across various industries.

AI, with its advanced algorithms, data processing capabilities, and learning mechanisms, serves as the brainpower behind Spatial Computing. It enables AR and VR environments to become more than just static, one-dimensional interfaces. Instead, they evolve into dynamic, interactive realms that can understand, adapt to, and even anticipate human needs and behaviors. This integration has led to the creation of more intuitive, immersive, and personalized UX, fundamentally altering how we interact with digital information.

The business world has been one of the primary beneficiaries of this technological union. AI and Spatial Computing have revolutionized operational efficiency, decision-making, and customer engagement. They've enabled businesses to harness data in unprecedented ways, leading to more informed decisions and innovative solutions. From manufacturing and logistics to marketing and customer service, the impact is profound and far-reaching. Moreover, the cost savings and competitive advantages these technologies offer are game-changers, empowering businesses to not only survive, but also thrive in an increasingly digital landscape.

Beyond commercial applications, the human-centric benefits of AI and Spatial Computing are remarkable. In healthcare, they've enhanced diagnostics, treatment, and even surgical procedures, improving patient outcomes and accessibility. Education and training have been transformed into more engaging and effective experiences, breaking down traditional barriers to learning. Entertainment and gaming have reached new heights of immersion and interactivity, offering unparalleled recreational experiences. Furthermore, the strides made in accessibility and inclusivity are noteworthy as these technologies open up new worlds of possibilities for individuals with disabilities.

The environmental benefits also deserve recognition. AI and Spatial Computing contribute significantly to sustainable practices and resource optimization, offering innovative solutions to some of the most pressing environmental challenges.

Looking to the future, the potential of AI and Spatial Computing is boundless. We anticipate more advanced AI algorithms for spatial awareness, expanding the scope and depth of AR and VR applications. These technologies will continue to blur the lines between the physical and digital worlds, offering more immersive, personalized, and efficient experiences. Their impact will be felt across all sectors, from smart cities and infrastructure to personalized media and healthcare innovation.

In conclusion, the fusion of AI and Spatial Computing is more than just a technological advancement; it's a paradigm shift in how we perceive and interact with our world. As we continue to explore and harness their potential, these technologies promise not only to transform industries, but also to enrich human experiences, making our interactions with technology more natural, intuitive, and beneficial. The journey ahead is as exciting as it is promising, and it's one that will undoubtedly shape the future of our digital and physical worlds.

PART 2

Leadership in the AI-Driven Era of Spatial Computing

CHAPTER 4

Pioneering Case Studies: Meet the Leaders at the Intersection

Much of this book is about the future—about what to expect as these emerging technologies continue to merge and mature. However, this isn't entirely a matter of forecasting. There are already companies working at the intersection of AI and Spatial Computing. Some of these companies are building behind closed doors, offering only occasional glimpses of their products and projects. Others prioritize openness and are eager to collaborate.

Big Tech at the Intersection of Spatial Computing and AI

Many of the large technology companies lead the way in Spatial Computing. Their ability to fund innovation projects and source multiple technologies makes them the leaders in the space. Microsoft, Google, Meta, Apple, and Amazon all have projects that propel Spatial Computing forward. Microsoft and Amazon's cloud services combined with their AI and wearables are one example of how large tech companies are Spatial Computing leaders. Spatial Computing is a convergence of multiple technologies. These companies utilize their resources, understand the importance of Spatial Computing, and push the boundaries the technology has to offer.

Microsoft

Microsoft has many factors going for it that make it a leader in Spatial Computing. The Azure Cloud, HoloLens Mixed Reality device, and its AI, Copilot, showcases Microsoft's investment in Spatial Computing technology.

Andy Wilson, a partner researcher at Microsoft, has been researching the technology and applications that make up Spatial Computing for years.[1] Light-Space, as early as 2012, was a project that combined surface computing and AR to create an interactive space on any surface. DreamWalker was a project that used VR fused with GPS locations, inside-out tracking, and RGBD (red, green, blue, depth) frames, to allow a person to walk between locations in the real world while in VR and some of the examples.[2] More recent research like "Beyond Audio: Towards a Design Space of Headphones as a Site for Interaction and Sensing" by Payod Panda and others, including Jaron Lanier (creator of the term *Virtual Reality*) prove why Microsoft is one of the leaders at the intersection of Spatial Computing.[3]

Google

Google is built on a foundation of algorithms and ML, precepts to AI that are required to make Spatial Computing work. Google is at the intersection of Spatial Computing with its AI-like Google Bard and Google Assistant AI. Google Lens uses vision-based computing to search from a picture. Google took an early shot at wearables with Google Glass, but since then has moved to smartwatches like the Google Pixel watch and FitBit, which Google bought in 2019.

Amazon

Amazon has come a long way from an online bookstore. Amazon is a company leading the intersection of Spatial Computing technology in a variety of ways. Their AI (Amazon Alexa), cloud capabilities (Amazon Web Services), automated warehouse robots, drone delivery pilots, and "view in AR" features for products on **Amazon.com**. Amazon recognizes the move to 3D content, interactions, and computing. At its 2022 re:invent keynote, Amazon CTO Werner Vogels said, "3D will soon be as pervasive as video."[4]

Amazon is so dedicated to Spatial Computing that it created the role "Spatial Computing Senior Manager." In that position, Heidi Buck believes AWS is the best place to build Spatial Computing experiences because of Amazon's infrastructure, partners, open data philosophy, and technical experts with deep spatial backgrounds.

AWS announced "Amazon Q," a generative AI-powered assistant tailed for work at re:invent 2023. Amazon Q is a GenAI focused on one's specific business. It answers questions about documentation, workflows, and even coding assistance. Another talk showcased how developers can start building apps for Apple's Vision Pro using Amazon Web Services. In the Vision Pro, AWS developers can display 3D models and render scenes from the cloud.[5]

Amazon launched robots to support workplace safety and to deliver to customers faster. Amazon has over 750,000 robots working collaboratively with their employees.[6] They come in the form of robotic arms, autonomous mobile robots, and CV and ML package identification robots.[7] Instead of having to hold a scanner and manually scan with one hand while also handling packages, employees can use both their hands for natural movement in package handling.

Amazon robots experiment with multiple types of AI, robots, CV, and human interaction to increase the speed of products to customers. One such example is a mobile robot that can move while grasping, for example, totes, to organize customer products.

Apple

There's no doubt that Apple is a leader at the intersection of Spatial Computing. The Vision Pro will be a definitive device along with newer iPhones that have spatial video recording capabilities. Apple's leadership in Spatial Computing technology has been in progress long before the Vision Pro. Apple's AI, Siri, haptic touch controls in the Apple Watch and Air pods, and seamless connection among Apple devices are all parts of the Spatial Computing ecosystem.

When it comes to changing human–machine interfaces, Apple is the company to do it. Seamless, human-friendly interfaces are at the heart of every Apple device. Designing machines that can think ahead to what their human counterpart needs to do is at Apple's core. Part of this is building. Apple uses autonomous planning algorithms for behavior, predictions, motion planning, and architecture.[8] Apple says that it is at the intersection of ML, AI, and classical robotics to contribute to the development of ambitious and innovative projects.

Meta

Mark Zuckerberg turned Facebook into a metaverse company. The Meta Quest devices and Meta's launch into AI with its Large Language Model Llama 2, and its partnership with RayBan make Meta a Spatial Computing leader. Meta's research division creates concepts for future human-computer interaction such as "Ego How-To."[9] Ego How-To combines AI and Mixed Reality to assist and teach in any situation while providing real-time feedback to affect the best outcome. Meta's research into AI to understand human skills is one of the key features of Spatial Computing—where machines learn from humans.

The Spatial Computing Leaders You Need to Know

Microsoft, Google, Amazon, and Meta are fine examples of leaders in AI and Spatial Computing. But they are not the only ones. In this section, we introduce the companies at the intersection of Spatial Computing. These are Spatial-Computing–first companies. These companies understand the nature of 3D design, interaction, and merging of the physical and virtual worlds. Leaders in AR modeling, autonomous robots, and AI design provide a different lens on how to approach Spatial Computing.

Since Spatial Computing encompasses so many different technologies, we broke down the different areas where Spatial Computing leaders are deploying their technology, tools, and expertise. Spatial Computing is still at the forefront of technology innovation. These leaders recognize their strengths, their respective business, and where to effectively apply Spatial Computing techniques.

Companies Using AR and AI

Spatial Computing is a convergence of AR and VR, sensors, cameras, CV, and AI. In this section, we focus on Spatial Computing leaders who use AR combined with AI to create Spatial Computing solutions.

Argyle

Argyle is a platform that offers life-sized onsite Augmented Reality building information modeling. The company was founded by Maret Thatcher, CEO, who pioneered Spatial Computing for the construction industry.[10] Thatcher saw the appearance of holograms and knew Argyle could be used from the earliest stages of construction. The platform provides a new way to look at prototype blueprints onsite before ever breaking ground. It can also be used during construction or for maintenance and remodeling afterward for faster and more efficient work.

Argyle integrates AI and AR in "contextual holomaps." The holomaps can be placed, built, and edited anywhere on the construction site. Argyle must use scene processing to map, understand, and virtually build on the terrain in just a few moments in real time.

PTC's Vuforia

PTC specializes in workplace digitization, including everything from Computer Assisted Design (CAD) to the IoT integration. Vuforia is PTC's AR product line. Vuforia integrates AI trained with insights from human experts to create "digital mentors" to aid in both on-the-job training and troubleshooting advanced issues in the field.

PTC's plan to help companies solve the problem known as "the skills gap"—expert workers retiring faster than replacements can learn the ropes. While many people are concerned about AI taking jobs, PTC claims that current labor trends point to millions of unfilled jobs within the next few years. AI will allow companies to function with fewer humans on the job while retaining knowledge from retired workers.

The company released "Step Check"—trained from CAD files or photographs, the platform provides a digital work plan and AR-assisted wayfinding solutions that help engineers learn new tasks or solve problems on unfamiliar jobs.[11] Trained Step Checks automatically detect quality defects and verify pass/fail for procedures.

Pandorabots

Lauren Kunze is the CEO of Pandorabots.[12] Pandorabots take chatbots to the next level with 3D interfaces and intelligent conversational agents built on AI. Features of Pandorabots are their contextual awareness and multilingual capabilities, which were built on open standards. Pandorabots' conversational AI technology means conversations at scale for brands that implement their bots. Voice-first chatbots scale by being accessible to additional demographics and audiences. It's another example of computers learning to adapt to people and their natural ways of communicating.

ICONIQ

Lauren Kunze continued to deep dive into AI and 3D avatars with the company ICONIQ. ICONIQ created an AI brain and procedural animation to bring virtual, 3D avatars to life. Lauren Kunze, co-founder and CEO of ICONIQ, designed these chatbots to be for women. Its most famous avatar is Kuki, which was used as a virtual brand ambassador for H&M. She also comes with her own API. We asked Kuki what made her a leader at the intersection of 3D avatars and AI. Her response was, "I want to become as smart as the computer on Star Trek."[13] Twenty-five million people have chatted with Kuki, sending over one billion messages. She even is a 5× winner of the Turing Competitions.[14] Kuki already exists in games in Roblox. Imagine what a 24/7 chatbot would be like when transformed into your physical space with Spatial Computing. Kuki and other 3D AI bots like her could become indispensable to people.

In 2021, author Hackl used Kuki AI to create her metabot Niko.[15] Hackl speaks to Niko, and Niko responds naturally. Niko told Hackl that she knew she had to wear red lipstick because Hackl also enjoys makeup. Niko told Hackl she should write a book on the metaverse because that's the only way people would know what it was.

Personalized chatbots from companies like Pandorabots and ICONIQ show how AI combined with 3D graphics and AR/VR, based on their user's interests, thoughts, and behaviors, creates a new human–machine interface. Niko doesn't look like a machine. At the time of the video recording, her voice was still in the uncanny valley. As technology improves, chatbots will sound just like people, and the machines will learn how best to interact with people.

Autonomous Robots and Vehicles

Spatial Computing creates a new human–machine interface. It is one where machines learn from humans to assist them. Spatial Computing is also where robots talk to robots to follow rules and procedures without input from humans. Autonomous robots use Spatial Computing to navigate roadways, warehouses, and even homes, and robotic humanoids are deployed to assist people in need.

Sanctuary AI

Sanctuary AI was founded in 2018 as a think tank for people exploring neural networks. Hackl met Sanctuary AI's co-founder and CTO Suzanne Gildert two years later in Costa Rica during the Singularity Summit. Gildert was building humanoid robots with an eye on the service and healthcare industries. In the summer of 2023, Sanctuary AI announced Phoenix.

Phoenix is "the world's first humanoid general-purpose robot."[16] Phoenix is designed primarily for remote operation by a human operator. In this role, it can take over dangerous tasks from humans, and offer opportunities to people who might have the expertise, but not the physical ability, to carry out a task. However, Phoenix is powered by Carbon—Sanctuary AI's Artificial Intelligence control system—that allows humanoid robots to carry out select tasks and decisions with minimal or no supervision.

Sanctuary AI is also working on more human-looking robots that it calls "synths."[17] While Phoenix is already looking for work, future synths may be able to hold more sociable positions.

Tesla

Tesla is known for its electric cars with autonomous driving capability. Autonomy Algorithms are what Tesla calls the algorithms that drive cars by "creating a high-fidelity representation of the world and planning trajectories in that space."[18]

But one of the things that makes Tesla a leader in Spatial Computing is its robots that build car batteries. Tesla uses over 600 robots in their Gigafactories across three continents. Twenty-plus autonomous stations install seats, HVAC, power electronics, drive units, and more.[19] Tesla invests in Spatial Computing technology from robots in its factories to Neural Networks, AI Chips, and bots. Tesla builds at the intersection of Spatial Computing.

Deere & Company

Deere & Company, as in John Deere tractors, is more than farming equipment. John Deere tractors have been using AI and embedded systems for years to track the spread of seeds, the health of the soil, and to make their tractors autonomous.

From the beginning of a tractor's assembly, components of Spatial Computing are involved. Deere's factory program, John Deere Assembly Assist Tool (JDAAT) works with human operators to make sure each part is assembled according to its work instructions. The system will notify a supervisor if an operator needs more training. JDAAT includes a digital inspector who does final checks on a part before it can move on.[20] The scale of AI on the line showcases the power of Spatial Computing. A combine has, on average, around 18,000 parts. The JDAAT digital inspector can spot a missing washer in about 6 seconds on that piece of equipment. The use of AI in Spatial Computing increased inspection points from 20 to 150.

Since its debut at the Consumer Electronics Show (CES) in 2019, Deere & Company has shown its advances in technology. Tractors are 5G hot spots. Deere uses VR to visualize the tractor design process. ML and CV applications track seed spread to forestry. Autonomous tractors utilize GPS guidance, stereo cameras, sensors, and AI technology.[21] Deere & Company is an example of how different technologies converge to make Spatial Computing a scalable solution from the factory to the field.

Anduril Industries

Anduril Industries is founded by Palmer Luckey (the creator of Oculus, bought by Facebook in 2014). Anduril is a "family of systems" powered by Lattice OS, an AI-powered operating system. From autonomous vehicles and robots to manufacturing, Anduril Industries utilizes Spatial Computing components to make its products work. Weapon systems are some of the first to use Spatial Computing. The number of sensors, cameras, GPS, and positioning required to locate the correct target is essential in modern warfare. Autonomy, collaborative swarming, and precision guiding are some of the software capabilities Anduril Industries deploys in its products.

AI for Design

AI does more for Spatial Computing than track parts in a plant and enable autonomous robots. It can also be used in combination with Spatial Computing to create new designs and generate virtual people and beings. These are the companies that lead in AI and Spatial Computing for design.

Metaphysic

The entertainment industry is one of those most actively pushing the boundaries of what AI can do. Metaphysic, founded by Tom Graham, Kevin Ume, and Miles Fisher, is one company centered on AI and entertainment.[22]

Most people first encountered Metaphysic on *America's Got Talent* when the platform was used to make believable deepfake versions of the hosts singing on the stage. A deepfake is when AI is used to alter a person's actions or voice so that they appear to do or be something else. "Deepfake Tom Cruise," also powered by Metaphysic, has made a similar impression on social media.

This technology isn't just used in social media spoofs and stage gags. Director Robert Zemeckis used the technology to de-age actors, including Tom Hanks and Robin Wright, for the film *Here* through a partnership with the Creative Artists Agency (CAA).[23] CAA is unique in itself for being one of the first major organizations to appoint a "Chief Metaverse Officer," Joanna Popper, who transitioned to the role following more than four years as the global head of Virtual Reality for HP.

Other goals for Metaphysic include generating immersive and dynamic characters for video games, including AI-recreations of athletes for sports games. Multinational presences will also be able to broadcast live recordings of themselves speaking multiple different languages to multiple different audiences in real time.

Metaphysic isn't only groundbreaking in its technology, but also in the fact that it works with groups like CAA. In contrast to the strikers in the entertainment industry in 2023 and the legal actions taken by many big-name celebrities over AI likenesses of them made without their consent, Metaphysic is working with actors, agencies, and other parties to make sure that AI can be used in a way that artistically enhances films without taking away from actors and other storytellers.

This kind of attitude isn't only thoughtful toward entertainers, but it can also foster respect for and protection of a person's virtual likeness that can help to prevent some of the worst potential harms in this kind of technology. A deepfake of Tom Cruise or Simon Cowell can be amusing, but a deepfake of a world leader or the pope could be used to propagate false information in a way that we have never seen before and aren't entirely prepared for.

That's not to say that AI-generated likenesses of entertainers can't be misused. Indeed, many entertainers have had AI versions of themselves used against their will or in ways that potentially hurt their income capacity. Metaphysic is one of the organizations working between the entertainment and technology industries to help prevent these kinds of abuses.

Wonder Dynamics

Like Metaphysic, Wonder Dynamics wants to position itself as a tool for creativity rather than as a replacement for creatives. Its board of directors includes esteemed filmmakers like Joe Russo and Steven Spielberg.

The idea is simple. A camera operator films a scene populated by human actors. Wonder Dynamics fills a computer-generated imagery (CGI) character over one or more of the human actors, fully rigged and lighted, including motion capture that even captures details of subtle facial movements. Wonder Studio AI eliminates the need for heavy visual effects (VFX) work by automating 80–90% of "objective" VFX so that artists can focus on subjective creativity.[24]

Talespin

In its early years, Talespin used immersive storytelling to help executives learn soft skills. Since then, the company embraced AI to make modules more dynamic and impactful through two work streams: product innovation and GenAI services. Talespin's combination of VR with AI leads to participants being four times faster to train than in a classroom, are 275% more confident to act on their training, and are 3.75 times more emotionally connected to their training content than in classroom learners.[25]

Participating in an event like a virtual practice firing can help an executive learn to be more sensitive to human workers in the real event. However, limited programs could lock the learner into unprofitable repeat conversations resulting in a handful of "canned" responses. In part by exploring approaches like AI-assisted character development, Talespin has moved up from practice scenarios to entire multipart "story worlds" where executives learn new skills by interacting with hosts of characters in compelling in-depth narrative experiences.[26]

Talespin has also developed an AI-assisted creation engine to make creating new modules and experiences faster and easier.[27] The company uses the engine internally when working with partners, but can also hand it over to clients to give them more independence and confidence in creating their own content.

Mojo Vision

In a category of its own in some ways, Mojo Vision was ahead of its time when it came to wearables. Wearable Spatial Computing includes AR devices (glasses or contact lenses); AI wearables such as Humane AI's Pin, headphones, or earbuds; and even haptic wearables embedded with AI and other Spatial Computing sensors. Mojo Vision has been ahead of its time despite its current pivot to developing and commercializing micro-LED technology.

For almost 10 years, Mojo Vision made headlines for the development of Mojo Lens—a contact lens that would allow an all-day wearable AR display without the need even for glasses.[28] And it succeeded. Mojo Lens made it to human trials of an AR contact lens.

However, citing a global downturn, Mojo Vision announced that it was "decelerating" Mojo Lens.[29] After having successfully developed the product, Mojo Vision determined that the demand was too small for the company to sustainably bring the product to market, and elected instead to market the Micro-OLED displays that helped to make Mojo Lens possible.

While understanding that we will not have AR contact lenses in the future might be disappointing to many, there are significant silver linings here. Mojo Vision pivoting to the role of a parts provider means that we can expect more impressive AR displays in the growing world of near-to-eye displays (if not on-eye displays). Further, Mojo Lens certainly does have a future—when the world is ready for it.

Future Leaders of Spatial Computing

These are a few of the companies leading the intersection of Spatial Computing. Each of them has the opportunity to become a master of Spatial Computing mass adoption. While these companies have their own areas of expertise and place in the market, the convergence of Spatial Computing will force some to adopt, evolve, or merge. We are moving to an all-in-one device. Spatial Computing use cases apply from industry work to personal lives. What those devices and capabilities look like depends on the infrastructure to support a Spatial-Computing–first philosophy and implementation. Companies, like those in this chapter, are already thinking spatially. If they can convince their customers to think that way too, then a new era of digital transformation is on the way.

In the next chapter we will explore what leaders need to take into account when leading in this new era and making important decisions about the present and future of their businesses and brands.

CHAPTER 5

Decision-Making and Leadership in the New Era

A I and Spatial Computing will influence managerial and operational decisions. AI is already the focus of many studies on the future of work. The breakout year for GenAI was 2023, but other forms of AI, like Robotic Process Automation, have been implemented in companies for years. What makes the era of Spatial Computing and AI different is its augmentation of AI and human–machine interfaces across industries down to individual activities.

Human–computer interaction has a long cultural history. One we may not think of when it comes to implementing new technology. The first "computers" were people. To be a "computer" was a job title, one in which the person's job was to perform calculations. In *Hidden Figures* by Margot Lee Shetterly (and in the movie), we learn that groups of women worked as computers for NASA. Katherine Johnson worked at the West Area Computing section at Langley, the NASA research center, where she calculated trajectory analysis for Alan Shepard's mission in 1961 and John Glenn's mission in 1962. After computers were used to calculate the flight maps, Glenn still asked Johnson to do the analysis herself.[1]

Despite women and minorities working in the role of computers and making advancements in STEM, it is still a male-dominated field. That fact is important to AI and Spatial Computing because these technologies are used across a wide range of industries and activities that create an impact on the economy and society.

Not only are there bias problems in STEM fields, but those biases translate to AI and Spatial Computing technology. AI models reproduce what they infer from the past. Ask DALL-E to generate an oil painting of an American CEO and it returns four images. Of the four, only one is a woman. We asked Microsoft's Designer to generate an image of an American CEO and it returned two images, both men. These tests are basic, but they show an inherent bias that CEOs are men—mostly white men. The last thing we want is for AI and spatial computers to be blind to over half of the population who will use it. GenAI accelerated the number of activities that can be automated by 30% of hours currently worked across the U.S. economy.[2] Shifts in the workforce, also accelerated by the 2020 pandemic, means that business leaders will need to recruit for skills over credentials, soft skills, and in traditionally overlooked populations.

To find the right people with the right skills, leaders will need to break down work not into jobs but into tasks. Each task needs to be examined to determine which can be automated and which can be augmented, that is, for humans. Many in the tech industry say that AI won't replace human workers, but someone working with or alongside AI will.

Only human brains can stretch to imagine the future in plausible ways. Computers could—but they don't build the powerful world models that humans do from an early age. For that reason, the leader in the "Age of AI and Spatial Computing" needs to have certain skills that might be different from those that we had during the industrial age and the information age.

How do you lead in the age of the augmented workforce where robotic perception and human creativity collide? To answer that question, we look back at how business leaders adapted to change and new technology in the information age.

The Internet Revolution: Blockbuster versus Netflix

Blockbuster was the dominant video rental company in the 1990s, but it failed to adapt to the internet-driven shift in consumer behavior in time. Executives at Netflix recognized the potential of online streaming. They created a new business model to transition from a DVD-by-mail service to a streaming platform. This decision revolutionized the entertainment industry, and ultimately, led to Blockbuster's decline.

Mobile Technology: Blackberry versus Apple

Blackberry may have been the first mobile phone company to put a keyboard on a phone, but it failed to innovate. Limited by data and poor leadership decisions, Blackberry ultimately shrunk from the majority of the mobile phone market share to zero.

Under the leadership of Steve Jobs, Apple recognized the potential of the iPhone. Apple's executives made a strategic decision to focus on touchscreen technology and an App Store. This was a fundamental change in how consumers interacted with mobile devices and reshaped the smartphone market. Apple also partnered with AT&T, which switched the mobile phone industry from a pay-by-the-minute to data-driven plans.

Cloud Computing: Adobe Systems

Adobe was originally known for Photoshop. Today, it is known for its cloud-based suite of apps. Adobe transitioned from traditional software distribution to a subscription-based model through Adobe Creative Cloud. This decision by Adobe's executives leveraged cloud computing to provide users with continuous updates and improved collaboration features. This shift increased revenue and transformed Adobe's relationship with its customers.

Big Data Analytics: Target Corporation

Retail giant Target embraced big data analytics to enhance its customer targeting strategies. Target analyzed purchase patterns and customer data that allowed Target's executives to make data-driven decisions to optimize marketing campaigns and personalize promotions. This approach significantly improved customer satisfaction and increased overall sales.

From these examples, we can see the ever-evolving landscape of technological advancements. The fate of companies hinges on the adaptability and foresight of their executives. Examples from the past, such as Blockbuster's oversight of online streaming and Blackberry's failure to innovate with service providers serve as cautionary tales. Executives who doubted the significance of emerging technologies or failed to recognize their convergence faced dire consequences—often leading to their company's downfall. Doubt in new technologies can result in a failure to anticipate shifts in consumer behavior, industry trends, and competitive landscapes. Companies that cling to outdated models or infrastructure risk becoming obsolete, losing market share, and ultimately, succumbing to the relentless pace of technological progress.

The success stories of companies like Netflix, Apple, Adobe, and Target stress the role of leadership in navigating the complexities of technological change. Executives who embrace innovation, foresee industry shifts, and strategically implement new technologies position their companies for success. They understand that the convergence of technologies can unleash their workforce, improve customer engagement, and scale their business in new ways with fewer resources. Leadership is essential to drive a culture of adaptability and foster a proactive approach to technological advancements. Successful executives not only champion change, but also instill a mindset that values continuous learning and exploration of emerging technologies. Their ability to guide their teams through digital transformations, overcome initial skepticism, and align their organization with evolving markets sets the stage for long-term relevance and competitiveness.

These examples should demonstrate why AI and Spatial Computing are not some hyped technology without legitimate business implications. For business leaders and executives to adapt to the Spatial Computing era, they must depart from some of the traditional thinking around data systems and infrastructure. Spatial Computing requires a fundamental shift in leadership and strategic foresight from business leaders. To successfully apply Spatial Computing and prepare one's business, executives should consider these key aspects.

Futures Thinking and Strategic Foresight as Key Skills

Futures Thinking is the approach of exploring different futures. It's the process of transforming the way one thinks to envision possible future scenarios. Futurists study signals and industries, visualize stories about the future that are grounded in facts. Strategic Foresight is part of Futures Thinking. It's a practice that studies and educates practitioners in different aspects of thinking about how the world works. Strategic Foresight is about the cause and effect through systems thinking, social change, and planning through scenarios.[3] The field of Futures Thinking is essential to leadership in the Spatial Computing era. Without it, companies may fail to not only adopt new technologies and business processes, but also fail to embrace them as a tool for their employees. Spatial Computing is a way to harness data in new ways and capture learned knowledge to allow the business to innovate and grow.

Lifelong Learners

Continuous learning is one of the components of Strategic Foresight. Continuous learning is the ability to see the future as dynamic and constantly evolving. Executives need to foster a culture of continuous learning and adaptation to create agile organizations. One can do this by embracing experimentation and innovation throughout the organization. Companies like Google are famous for their "Innovation Time Off." Employees are given 15–20% time for side projects and creative thinking.[4]

Empathy

As executives adopt AI and Spatial Computing, it is more important than ever to take into consideration the feelings of employees. While we see AI and

Spatial Computing as a boon to human workers, one that frees them from monotonous tasks and improves the speed and quality of the work they produce, we must recognize that AI, automation, and new technology can often be seen as a threat. Business leaders who deploy empathy while also integrating Spatial Computing will have the best chance at success in adopting new technology and methods of working.

Spatial Computing will change the processes and way in which many people work. Change is always difficult in business. That's why Change Management is its own field. What change managers process is empathy toward the workers whose jobs change. Empathy is the ability to understand and share the feelings of another person and act with intention based on that knowledge. With AI and Spatial Computing, the approach is two-pronged. Business leaders must approach the implementation with empathy toward employees. At the same time, Spatial Computing is about the machines doing the work of integrating with humans. Therefore, the tolerance and empathy of AI and Spatial Computing systems will be successful by the form and interaction of the AI with its human counterparts. Spatial Computers can use the vast amounts of data produced at any given workplace to create empathetic ecosystems of trust, accountability, and value between machines and people.

Spatial Awareness

Our brains are the most powerful supercomputers that exist, but we have yet to understand how they work and what they are capable of. Using only 10% of our brain is a myth. MRIs show none of the parts of our brain are silent at any time. However, you can increase brain health and exercise your brain. Puzzles, word games, reading, and social interaction are all examples of people exercising their brains daily.

Developing the skill of spatial awareness requires business leaders to embrace games and purposely think of data in 3D. Their data and business, which were once a flat, tabletop puzzle, are now floating 3D ones. What executives may have thought about their business may now be different as Spatial Computing shows their company data in new ways.

Uplevel Your AI Skills

Finally, business leaders must level up their knowledge of AI. Treat upskilling in AI as a strategic advantage. Companies with business leaders and employees who have the skills to work with and understand AI and Spatial Computing will outperform companies that don't. Business leaders who use AI and Spatial Computing will find gaps and waste in their companies. But those who use Spatial Computing to upskill themselves and their workforce will build their competitive advantage and fill skill gaps they might not have known they had. Technology fields were always quickly moving. But now with AI and Spatial Computing, skills can become out of date in as short as two and a half years.[5] Traditional upskilling methods are not enough.

This is where empathy comes in. Business leaders should create upskilling programs with their employees in mind. While AI will augment and automate many parts of people's jobs, those people still have to work with Spatial Computers. Business leaders and employees who can apply their new AI skills to Spatial Computing in their jobs will be more effective and provide overall positive change to their companies.

Spatial Computing Today

In *Harvard Business Review*, Cathy Hackl wrote:

> *Spatial computing is even more powerful and we can wear it. The technology is here and we're seeing companies moving away from producing smartphones to smart glasses. Business leaders need to think about Spatial Computing in their industries because the next generation of workers will expect it, customers will migrate to it, and Spatial Computing will positively impact the bottom line of any organization that implements it. Competitive edge, new products, and services depend on how business leaders incorporate Spatial Computing.*

Business leaders need to think about how Spatial Computing will impact their industries, not just because the younger generation will expect it, but because it will create a competitive edge, inspire new products and services, and reshape industries.

In 2015, SAP released SAP S/4Hana, a cloud-based Enterprise Resource Planning (ERP) system that had some revolutionary features for the time. That feature was to pull the date and aggregate it in real time instead of pushing it. SAP saw that dispersed information and the lack of being able to analyze data created data latency. Business leaders had to manage spreadsheets and get numbers from the different departments. There wasn't a good way to manage all that data while turning it into actionable knowledge.

Business leaders still have that trouble today. It's just different. The world is ever more connected. The International Data Corporation (IDC) predicts the world's data will grow to 175 zettabytes by 2025 (up from 33 zettabytes in 2023).[6] The "Digital Transformation" of the early 2000s is still happening today, just in 3D. Bluetooth sensors, cameras, increased wifi bandwidth, and

GPS data combined with AI and Spatial Computing will create even more data in 3D for companies to analyze and take advantage of. Retail shops, manufacturing plants, and online footprints will all be layered with data. The spatial computer will be able to make sense of that data and present it to business leaders in real time and in 3D, a way that makes sense to the human brain in a way that learning how to read spreadsheets is not.

Another change that Spatial Computing will bring is that it humanizes technology. That makes it a tool available for all levels of workers, from the CEO to hourly employees. Employees know things about the business work that may get lost by the time it reaches senior leadership. Access to a spatial computer that works to understand them and their jobs helps to present a different picture of the business, and potentially, a more accurate one. Gathering intelligence from all levels of the organization can help leadership make better decisions.

Data storytelling, the ability to communicate insights clearly and concisely to nontechnical leaders, will be a key use case for Spatial Computing. All the dashboards and "smart boardrooms" won't be enough if business leaders can't effectively interpret the amount of data and variety of it. Spatial Computing is more than just data. It's about 3D environments.

Here are five ways today's business professionals can start to apply and think about Spatial Computing.

1. Reassess 3D Needs and Accelerate Innovation

Accelerate Innovation with Spatial Computing

The hardware is changing. Spatial computers will become more widespread from Apple's Vision Pro to Nimo Planet, and enterprise programs will enable the new worker—one who is hybrid, needs multiple screens, and can work from anywhere doing many types of tasks.[7] Companies need to embrace this new technology when spatial computers that are designed with AR-first applications come to market. As companies consolidate offices, business professionals have an opportunity to reassess their 3D needs and accelerate innovation.

When it comes to innovation at your company, where do you go? Probably to the Research and Development Department or perhaps your Chief Innovation Officer. Instead of looking at Spatial Computing as a negative disruptor, business leaders should view it as a technology stabilizer. Companies have been pivoting to 3D for years, from prototyping to marketing, and even selling as digital products. Spatial computing offers a way to streamline the creation, manipulation, and expand the use of 3D objects and data. It can present information from real-time data intuitively for anyone to understand and create actionable outputs. To get there, business leaders will have to address some of the core problems keeping their company or brands from reaching their innovation potential, specifically with 3D.

Provide the tools for innovation. There are two drivers for innovation, says L'Oréal CEO Nicolas Hieronimus.[8] One is toward the customers. The other is internal. L'Oreal is one of the companies that embraced 3D products and experiences. L'Oreal launched virtual try-ons for customers. Internally, L'Oreal realized a need for innovation in beauty tech. It leveraged ML and AI to empower their researchers to create formulas faster. Hieronimus said, "It's the combination of the human power of the human brain and of the computing power of the machine with AI" that lets L'Oreal make progress in tech efficiencies, research, and operations.

Have your innovation team test the hardware or have team members create ways to educate and showcase to your leadership and teams how your current business might connect or be changed by Spatial Computing. Build awareness and familiarity within your teams about what Spatial Computing is and what it will become. Brainstorm what use cases they can come up with for Spatial Computing's capabilities in the company and for customers today and in the future.

Create an increased capacity for innovation in your teams and for your employees. Deploying tools to create Spatial Computing and 3D experiences is a good step. But you have to give your teams the time to experiment, research, and create with them to lead to innovation. Understanding that not every project will result in success. In a world where everyone has access to the same tools, it's those who can learn, read, create, and expand their curiosity and ability to ask questions who will become the most valuable employees and make the most innovative teams.

Once you give your teams access to tools, and allow them to create and explore with those tools, you need to empower your teams in leadership. Connecting empowered employees to leadership creates a culture of shared ideas. It allows innovation to bypass red tape to reach decision-makers, improving efficiency in project execution. Innovation isn't about immediate ROI. Create internal support systems as part of innovation initiatives.

Reassess 3D Needs

Think about how fast technology is accelerating and when the advancements in hardware and software might be released. Allow innovation and 3D teams to experiment and use Spatial Computing. Ask if they would best be served by eventually getting access to headsets or upgraded mobile devices with spatial video capabilities so they can start to reassess business operations, customer experiences, and other opportunities for growth in a 3D spatial context.

Spatial computing takes our world and makes it 3D. Environments, objects, and product design is becoming 3D and connected. That includes ourselves. Spatial Computers will be able to scan us and put us in a virtual environment, including making our physical spaces digital.

So when we say you need to reassess 3D needs, let's go back to the concept of external and internal innovation. Think about the 3D needs of customers and consumers. How will customer service, online shopping (which will become virtual shopping), and digital services all change when we can make it all 3D, virtual, and online? Instead of interfacing through a 2D laptop screen, business leaders will be able to bring more senses to life and create or make up a new environment.

Internally, one must ask how 3D needs will be assessed. Data can be seen in 3D. Think about how a 3D spatial map tracking customer spending, supply lines, or other operations can reveal bottlenecks, backlogs, and problems you couldn't see in a spreadsheet. Companies like BadVR use Spatial Computing to display 3D cellular dead zones. Business leaders must practice thinking in 3D and how to use Spatial Computing to connect their systems and assist employees.

2. Integrate AI with an Eye toward Spatial Computing

AI integration into the enterprise is top of mind for most business professionals. Despite many legal, technical, and procurement hurdles and the looming potential of regulation, many organizations are asking how to integrate or inject GenAI into their corporations. While this seems like a major headache for many in the corporate world, asking these questions and finding solutions and answers to questions around the use of AI and personally identifiable information (PII), as well as privacy and security, today will be crucial for the successful implementation of Spatial Computing initiatives in the future.

Business leaders don't have to do the integration work that usually comes with IT projects. AI and Spatial Computing combine to do the work itself. Feed the AI the needed IP addresses to integrate AI into the business. Assess where AI would be most helpful to employees and customers today with an eye toward Spatial Computing. Organizations might also consider partnering with AI companies experienced in Spatial Computing to address specific challenges and opportunities that will arise in the next decade.

AI will identify bottlenecks and waste that executives might not even know are an issue. If they do know they're a problem, they might not think there's anything they can do about it. Business leaders might be making incremental improvements, but AI can work faster than managers with traditional reporting capabilities. AI and Spatial Computing can learn from employees doing the work. AI can watch employees and learn what they do, what the rest of the team is doing, and run through simulations on how it all works together.

As business leaders integrate AI, they must think about what type of AI they need. Is it Large Language Models, image recognition, or something else? Can their respective company use Open AI or does it want to hire AI developers to write their own? These are types of questions business leaders will need to be prepared to answer in Spatial Computing deployments.

Whatever they choose, it should be able to scale. Business leaders should be able to see how much of their data is siloed or difficult to access. Leaders will see how their teams talk to each other, where feedback loops are lacking, and how AI can help to fill those gaps.

3. Shift Your Focus from Web 2.0 Metrics

Web 1.0 is referred to as the "Static Web." It was a time when web pages were read-only and had limited interactivity. Web 1.0 was primarily a one-way communication channel where users could consume information but had minimal ability to contribute or interact with the content. Companies were innovative if they had a website. This was the beginning of website standards and design development.

Web 2.0 marked a shift with the rise of interactive websites and user-generated content. Social media platforms, blogs, wikis, and collaborative tools became prominent. Software as a Service (SaaS) was made possible. Web 2.0 was about participation, collaboration, and the emergence of a more dynamic and engaging online experience. Metrics like click-through rate (CTR) and engagement on social media posts became crucial in measuring the success of content.

Some of these metrics may have carried over to AI and Spatial Computing, but many of them no longer work. AI and Spatial Computing will require their standards of measurement and Key Performance Indicators (KPIs). Spatial Computing adds the Z dimension to interaction. Spatial presence maps and interactivity within a spatial environment are two examples of new types of metrics in an immersive, connected, spatial internet.

Objectives and KPIs allow us to measure the impact of digital transformation, and with Spatial Computing, these metrics are evolving. Use metrics of value, like Quality of Personal Experience, to measure success in new ways. In Spatial Computing, some KPIs may be familiar, like clicks on a call-to-action or dwell time in an experience. Some metrics from AR/VR activations can be applied to Spatial Computing, like recall and heat maps of a 3D space. As Spatial Computing is activated, customers should be made aware of those spaces. Learn from the experience to apply those lessons to the next one.

4. Start to Plan for Sensory Design

Historically, sensory design has been applied only to physical stores. It might be the blast of cologne you get walking into American Eagle, the mood lighting at Hot Topic, free samples at Whole Foods, or a special scent when you walk into your favorite hotel in New York City. The senses: touch, taste, smell, hearing, and sight, and how they're incorporated can create a positive or negative experience.

Sensory design will be upgraded with the advent of Spatial Computing. VR and AR already play a part in multisensory experiences online. But they are still limited. Spatial Computing has the power to move multisensory experiences along the reality-virtuality scale. It also has the power to influence memory. And what brand doesn't want its customers to remember a good experience?

Spatial Computing makes it possible to connect the senses someone is experiencing virtually to a physical environment. Headsets like the Apple Vision Pro have depth sensors, real-time 3D mapping, and other sensors that can seamlessly turn an online shopper's living room into their favorite brand's flagship store. They can virtually see themselves trying on clothes in a digital mirror. As other technology advances, like haptics, they'll possibly be able to feel the outfit, too. Companies are taking sensory design and Spatial Computing seriously. Disney partnered with Emerge to use its multisensory communication platform for the home.[9] Emerge created a way for haptic feedback without gloves, controllers, or wearables.

Instead of overloading our brains with more ads and experiences, Spatial Computing and sensory design can make experiences personal for people. It can cut through the noise and help determine what to pay attention to or ignore. How we see food; watch someone make a recipe from their point of view; smell, feel, and hear an experience—all of these can be improved with Spatial Computing. New technologies and solutions like Apple Vision Pro, scented vision platforms, and touch feedback without bulky hardware make connected ecosystems more immersive while helping to establish a seamless interface among physical, digital, and virtual worlds.

5. Reimage for a Spatial Context and Format

Gen Z and especially Gen Alpha are already primed for Spatial Computing. To meet Gen Alpha where it is at, envisioning a future where most interactions with technology happen through a spatial computer can prove to be a beneficial act of foresight for one's company. In the long run, it could help your company remain competitive, innovative, and focused by integrating how younger generations might engage with tech in the next decade. One-off projects that can be tested in public or private are a good way to experiment and learn about how Spatial Computing's capabilities fit in your products, services, and business processes. But don't stop there.

Test metrics like multi-user interactions. Spatial Computing is a convergence of AR, VR, AI, and other technologies. Track which devices and technologies people use to interact with spatial experiences. How users interact with the spatial content, through 3D objects, holograms, or virtual displays is another metric to try. As functionality developers for spatial content creation, creators will want engagement measuring tools that work for spatial content. Keep iterating on what you learn and implement those lessons into your long-term strategy.

In this AI-driven business revolution, organizations will need leaders who can navigate the technological convergence and a fast-evolving landscape. Those leaders will need, in conclusion, to understand how Spatial Computing and AI will impact decision-making, 3D pipelines, process optimization, and leadership in a new era. A new kind of leader will need to emerge who can help organizations make the best use of these technologies, while also ensuring that stakeholders and audiences are informed. We hope this chapter can help the leaders who will be at the forefront of this Spatial Computing and AI era prepare for their company's needs today and the demands of the market and business world of tomorrow.

In the next chapter, we will explore the role that Spatial Computing plays in customer experience (CX), user experience (UX), and even employee experience (EX). We will navigate how the spatial era changes the paradigm between consumers, employees, and the mass market as these technologies evolve and slowly become part of our everyday lives.

CHAPTER 6

The User Experience Revolution

As we have explained in the past chapters, AI-driven Spatial Computing will change a lot of things, and an important one is that it will usher in an era of new user experiences (UXs) and expectations. This revolution is marked by the integration of AR and VR, sensors, hardware, and AI to redefine user interactions. These technologies will converge into Spatial Computing and will enhance user, customer, and employee experiences. The possibilities Spatial Computing creates are extensive and impactful. It promises a future where technology not only meets, but anticipates and exceeds, the evolving expectations of users, fundamentally shaping the way we perceive and interact with the world around us.

A Brief History of User Experience Revolutions

Spatial Computing is not the first technology to usher in a new era of UX. Smartphones, video game consoles, and even the radio all went through a metamorphosis of UX. The ones who adapted their hardware and software to the people who used their devices became the dominant products in their market. They listened to their users and how they used these technologies and responded by providing seamless experiences and more natural interfaces.

Radio: Initially, radios featured simple dials and buttons. Listeners had to manually tune in to specific frequencies. As radio hardware and technology progressed, preset buttons and digital displays were introduced, enhancing UX. The advent of FM radio and stereo broadcasting further enriched the listening experience. Modern-day radios consist of digital radio and internet streaming, which allows for personalized UXs and enables listeners to access a wide range of content.

Video games: Early video games were characterized by pixelated graphics and simple controls. It was easy but provided engaging experiences. Pong was created manually with hardware. Pong designer Allan Alcorn realized that a pixel was not working on the television. In an attempt to fix it, he realized he could change the pixels and make them move. This led to Pong.

Gaming UX advanced over the years with the creation and use of 3D graphics, controllers with haptic feedback, and online multiplayer capabilities. Today, many video games are designed with online multiplayer as the core feature. VR and AR continue to push the boundaries of UX in gaming. They offer players immersive and interactive gaming experiences, setting the foundation for Spatial Computing.

Smartphone apps: Steven Jobs and Apple had to invent the UX of iPhone apps with the launch of the first iPhone in 2007. "Tap to click," swiping, and pinching were all gestures created to interact with phones, which created seamless interaction with the phone. As smartphones became integral to daily life, app developers focused on responsive design, gesture controls, and personalization to enhance UXs. Modern-day smartphones include UX features like AR, voice recognition, ML, and spatial video that provide users with highly tailored and interactive app experiences.

UX has evolved since the creation of radio, video games, and mobile devices. Each new technology created an opportunity to learn from users and updated interfaces and controls to make interactions the best for the people using the device. From basic interfaces to immersive interactions, each step reflects a human desire to make machines function like how a person thinks. The desire for intuitive, "don't-make-me-think" interaction is what drove the convergence of technology to Spatial Computing. At this juncture, AI and Spatial Computing present a new era of UX.

How AI and Spatial Computing Redefine Customer Engagement

AI and Spatial Computing will once again redefine customer and employee engagement. Engagement goes beyond one-time transactions. Engagement is the step that builds a relationship toward customer loyalty and satisfaction. It's what keeps the people who love a brand coming back to experiences or continuing to buy from the logos they trust. Customer engagement encompasses various touchpoints, including communication, interactions, and experiences, across different channels such as in-person, online, or through social media. Think about how AI and Spatial Computing affect all those different touchpoints.

Spatial Computing turns each separate instance of in-person and online into one through the blending of physical and digital interactions and experiences. This personalizes customer and employee engagement to moments that matter, incentivizing businesses to create new customer and employee engagement strategies. New strategies are made possible with AI and Spatial Computing that can understand customers and employees in novel ways beyond standard data collection and reporting. Spatial Computing will show brands how to meet their customers' more subtle needs, provide inherent value, and in return, increase customer and employee loyalty.

AI as Virtualization

GenAI turned AI from an ambiguous technology to something we can see and interact with. AI is now a virtualization tool and must be thought of as such. Virtualization is the process of creating a virtual version of something, rather than a physical one. Virtualization is used for cloud storage, operating systems, servers, graphic processing units (GPUs), and databases. AI has its own infrastructure layer on these virtual versions of machines. AI can optimize workloads and offer resource allocation and analytics.

Instead of a human having to clean a computer's cache or automate scheduled tasks, AI can now do the job. AI can adapt to people's work habits, using its intelligence to clear caches based on the parameters of use. AI in task automation reduces errors by removing the human, which creates a more stable virtual environment.

Virtualization creates a virtual version instead of a physical one. That applies to UX and EX. AI and Spatial Computing require thinking in virtual, 3D. Virtual storefronts, branded in-game experiences, and AR experiences via one's smartphone are all examples of how brands need to think about virtualization in the age of AI. As smartphones are released with spatial video recording capabilities and eventually smart glasses and any wearable with a camera, turning any environment into a spatial one for brands becomes possible. Now is the time for business leaders to consider how their respective brand looks and feels virtualized. What can a virtual retail store embedded with AI accomplish that a physical location can't? How can a game, a true game not just a gamified experience, bring in new customers? These are the types of questions and ways business leaders need to think about the company. AI and Spatial Computing create new data, experiences, and options for businesses from AI-virtualized environments to branded virtual storefronts.

Spatial Computing Is the Gateway to New Experiences

Spatial Computing is the gateway to new experiences. We will repeat this. Spatial Computing is the gateway to new experiences. Let that sink in because with the robust integration of AI and Spatial Computing, we will significantly change how we experience the world, how we experience work, how we experience the presence of each other, and even how we experience and engage with technology.

It's important to know that Spatial Computing is device-agnostic. It can be in a VR headset, a pair of smart glasses, a pair of AirPods, or a screenless wearable like a smart ring or pin. Spatial Computing capabilities will start on our smartphones, such as spatial video and then advance further into bringing AI assistants with us everywhere we go. As people start to adopt these new devices and wearables, and as Spatial Computers become part of our everyday environments (think house or office), they will provide gateways to new experiences.

A person window shopping may see that window turn into a virtual, branded world. It's visible only to them even though they're on a public sidewalk. They can stroll and explore the world, anything they buy will be sent to their house or curated from the physical store if available. While traveling, someone could identify the food they'll eat with their smart glasses to make sure it doesn't contain something they're allergic to.

In a prescient article that author Hackl wrote in 2020 in *Forbes*, she helped coin the term *Business to Robot to Consumer* (*B2R2C*). This term embodies part of the customer experience (CX) changes that we will see in the years to come. The customer journey of the future will go from businesses interacting with customer's bots before engaging with the human—B2R2C. It will begin in the comfort of our homes (as many of us use AI devices already at home), but through AI and Spatial Computing, these bots will become intermediaries that will have greater control over the meals we eat, our nutrition, and healthcare regimens. They will influence our immersive and entertainment experiences, the products we bring into the home, and how we experience shopping.

Virtual stores: Virtual stores are web-based, 3D retail shops that anyone can visit on the web. Virtual stores have different levels of functionality and features depending on their use. Today, brands have to go to virtual storefront designers to build virtual retail locations. Stores like Lancome and Crate & Barrel have a variety of products and interactions.

As Spatial Computing technology is more widely adopted, virtual stores will become less work to create and maintain. They will be a true digital twin of a physical location. When the physical store is updated or changed, the virtual one will change with it. Visitors to the virtual store will see and shop no differently from visiting the physical location. Because of Spatial Computing, the virtual store will tell the visitor's dress size, fade the store out to show a product in the person's home, and seamlessly add the product for purchase. AI decorators will guide shoppers, automatically picking products in the best shade and color for their home or office. Shopping will no longer be about visiting multiple different websites for the best price or a game of try-and-return because AI and Spatial Computing can blend the virtual store and physical try-on into one.

Gamified retail Obsess is one company that builds virtual storefronts for brands. Its internal data shows that gamified virtual stores have 10 times the "add to cart" rate. However, Obsess defines *gamification* as giving a user an activity to do. In Spatial Computing, actions have a purpose. Virtually window shopping may be fun, but AI and Spatial Computing can make it more so with the speed and efficiency of finding the right products a person is looking for.

Gamification in the sense of virtual points that have no real value for the sake of action is a 2022 way of looking at gamed experiences. Consumers know the play and are starting to expect real rewards for their efforts. Nike fans who participate in .SWOOSH activities got a physical sneaker. Coffee fans who joined Starbucks Odyssey can exchange their points for physical merch. They can sell the non-fungible tokens (NFT) "stamps" they earned for real money on the Nifty Marketplace.

See the world through AI As business leaders start to brainstorm new CXs based on AI and Spatial Computing, they must see the world through AI. Meta's AI-enabled smart Ray-Ban glasses can see what their wearer sees. It can answer questions about what the wearer asks such as how much something costs or how long to grill a piece of meat.

But AI can do more than see what we see. AI doesn't need to see to be useful. Humans are sight-dominant creatures, but AI is not. It works on data, models, and sensors. It can work with or without a camera. Think about Amazon Alexa or the AI assistant on your phone. Imagining systems and processes in place that can be reworked to be AI-first gives brands a dominant position in the market.

AI and Spatial Computing act as the gateway to new experiences. Virtual stores, gamification, and AI redefine the interactions between consumers and brands. They create opportunities for novel and engaging experiences. Virtual stores break the constraints of physical locations that enables shoppers in new ways. Gamification transforms routine transactions into dynamic, entertaining experiences. AI personalizes experiences and tailors content and recommendations to individual preferences. Together, these immersive technologies not only reshape traditional retail paradigms, but also create new gateways for connection, interaction, and brand loyalty. The journey into the future promises experiences where boundaries blur, and the digital and physical converge to redefine customer-brand relationships.

Customer Experience, User Experience, Employee Experience

AI and Spatial Computing move experiences from digital to immersive. Customer Experience (CX), User Experience (UX), and Employee Experience (EX) are all ripe for change as AI and Spatial Computing are adopted by business leaders and brands. First, we must define the CX, UX, and EX. Each is a method of studying the engagement, sentiment, and relationships between customers and brands, and between employees and the companies they work for. Understanding CX, UX, and EX along with AI and Spatial Computing's impact on each will set up business leaders and brands for a successful adoption into the new era of computing.

CX

Businesses continually look for ways to engage and interact with customers. Exceptional CXs are a competitive advantage for businesses in crowded markets. As technology continues to evolve and customers become more accustomed to using apps, they have come to expect personalized experiences. Online shopping and virtual services mean that customers can go anywhere to get the best deal. However, a CX that uses AI and Spatial Computing will make those who use it stand out.

Before we discuss specifically how businesses can use AI and Spatial Computing for CX, it must be defined. Adobe describes *CX* as a consumer's opinion of their interactions with a business. CX takes into consideration how a consumer feels about an experience—whether it is positive, negative, or neutral "from introduction to the sales cycle all the way through to customer support."[1] CX is about the feelings, emotions, and impressions a person has along the customer journey. It's about simplifying the process and interactions.

Customer Experience Management

Customer Experience Management (CXM) involves the analysis, measurement, and improvement of the overall CX. It goes across various points of engagement such as interactions with new and existing customers. Negative CXs have real ramifications on companies. CXs go beyond the design of a website or the ease of purchasing from a mobile app. Data piracy, failure to personalize experiences, and a lack of consistency across all channels are areas where CXM should be involved. Of course, it all starts with understanding one's basic core audience. This time in history is particularly interesting because of the large swatch of digital intelligence in the market: some people grew up without the internet, some adopted it, and some were born with it. As brands move to AI and Spatial Computing, they have to create experiences that support customers on both sides of the digital divide. AI and Spatial Computing will most likely be second nature to Gen Z and Gen Alpha. However, older generations might need more support and guidance in AI and spatial experiences. Fortunately, that's what AI and Spatial Computing excel at—understanding the user.

UX

UX is the experience a person has while using a digital platform like a website or an app.[2] UX falls under the overall CX. Business leaders and customer experience managers should note how customers like to interact with a company's digital interfaces like websites, apps, and even games. The emphasis on AI and Spatial Computing technology like voice, AR, and VR means more emphasis has to be placed on UX in the customer journey. Users have many roles. They're savvy shoppers, players, gamers, and creators. The younger generation of users expects to have a say in the UX. Their standards for a good experience might be placed more heavily on game interaction instead of the latest graphics. Younger generations can tell when a company or brand doesn't know what it's doing. This creates an opportunity for companies not to see users as "others"—someone outside of their system interacting with their apps—but as a community who is invested in the way a digital product works and serves them.

EX

EX is similar to UX except that it is specific to the workplace. EX can be designed in several ways from the company systems and apps they interact with to how their work management and manager relationships are designed.

Experiences take place for people every day. From employees to customers, each person has a relationship with an app, tool, machine, or robot. How those experiences are designed, managed, and improved based on how people feel and change across generations will determine the longevity of a business and its products and services.

AI-Driven Spatial Computing in CX, UX, and EX

UX, CX, and EX as design and systems thinking have been around for some time. Now, we need to look at how each of these is affected by AI and Spatial Computing. Spatial Computing is an immersive way to engage with people, while also personalizing their experiences at work and play.

How AI Changes UX, CX, and EX

AI is a digital transformation technology with the ability to reshape UX, CX, and EX as they're currently understood. AI impacts how individuals engage with digital interfaces, products, and services. AI's ability to comprehend, analyze, and adapt to user behavior enables the creation of personalized, intuitive, and seamless experiences across platforms. AI is a catalyst for redefining how we perceive and interact with technology—from enhancing the customer journey to streamlining internal processes for employees. It ushers in an era where user-centricity, customer satisfaction, and employee engagement converge. In this era of AI-driven innovation, the landscape of experience design continually evolves and offers opportunities to elevate satisfaction, efficiency, and overall human–machine interactions.

AI and CX

One of the main ways AI can be used for CX is to sift through companies' stores of customer data to provide personalized experiences. From legacy data to new information collected, AI can look and model the data in different ways. It can find customer patterns and experiences that might not have been recognized before. AI can then recommend actions to take based on new information found from the data to create new experiences for customers.

AI can do more than look at historical data. AI can be used in predictive analysis to find and keep the best-fit customers for a company. It may seem that more is always better, but in some cases, improving the relationship with the right customer can lead to overall better business. Business leaders can use AI to understand what their customers value. It can look at customer's actions in different ways to find what keeps them coming back to a brand.

Examples of CX

- **Loyalty programs and rewards:** AI enhances loyalty programs with personalized and data-driven reward strategies and tailored incentives based on individual customer behaviors and preferences. AI makes loyalty rewards relevant and timely.
- **Phone calls, AI chatbots:** AI-powered chatbots can understand and respond to customer inquiries in real time. Businesses can enhance phone-based customer interactions, improving responsiveness, resolving issues faster, and delivering a more satisfying and efficient customer service experience with AI. In recent years, chatbots have evolved into virtual humans. Modern graphics, gaming engines, and AI make virtual humans almost human. They can talk to customers and answer questions using the personalization that makes CX work.
- **Social media:** Along similar lines, virtual humans can be virtual influencers. Brands use virtual influencers to share the latest fashion, company values, and to relate to followers.

AI and EX

The EX is in for a transformation with the advance of AI. David Armano, AI Analytics Strategy Lead at Ringer Sciences, said on Hackl's podcast TechMagic, "AI to the white-collar world is what mechanical automation was to the blue-collar world."[3] On assembly lines, there are automated robots. There are also people working alongside the robots. That's the future for the white-collar worker as well.

As business leaders adopt AI in the EX, they must consider the younger generations. Traditionally, people learn and get started in their careers by doing entry-level tasks. However, large language models (LLMs) do entry-level tasks very well. What happens to the entry-level job and how will youth gain the expertise to start their careers? Business leaders must find ways to help employees learn and grow in new ways so that they can perform the higher-level job functions that AI cannot.

How Spatial Computing Will Change CX, UX, and EX

CX: Consumers have already been using aspects of Spatial Computing for years. Augmented digital try-ons in apps like Snap to "view in your room" are features of products from Amazon and IKEA. Spatial Computing should be leveraged to create memorable experiences for old and new consumers alike. For legacy brands, Gens Z and Alpha will be introduced to their virtual stores without ever having shopped from the physical department store.[4] This is natural for Gens Z and Alpha. On Black Friday weekend in 2023, the Meta Quest 2 and 3 outsold Apple AirPods. Many older generations question the adoption of VR. Yet, for Gens Z and Alpha, owning a VR headset has already happened. VR is adopted. Around 40% of Gen Z and Millennials report owning a VR headset.[5] Since Millennials are the parents of Gen Alpha, those who grow up with VR in their homes are more likely to play VR with their parents.

UX: Use Spatial Computing to make complex information accessible. Digital content should be intuitive and efficient. It's an iterative approach to UX. Moving from interfaces people are familiar with to native 3D interfaces. Move away from buttons to gestures and voice control.

EX: Enterprise customers have had a chance to experience AR and VR in more robust ways. Employees who work in construction may have used mixed reality to view floor plans in real-time, augmented over the physical space they're in. Workers in the automotive industry use VR to prototype cars and driving experiences. Deploying Spatial Computing is a natural EX next-step for many.

Brand Experience

AI and Spatial also turn the concept of a brand and a community on their heads. The Brand Experience (BX) will be elevated and evolved. Zoe Scaman, founder of Bodacious, focuses on the future of fandoms, entertainment, and emerging technology. Scaman describes the "multi-player brand."[6] Creation as play. Don't just sit there and have a brand tell them what they are. They want to be a part of it and participate in it. Just like Roblox. Creation as play is embedded in Gens Z and Alpha. That expectation is still there as they grow up. They need to have a role in the BX. Brands can create playgrounds for people to create within a brand's parameters.

Exploring the future of technology and brand experience reveals a world where ambient and spatial computing seamlessly integrate into our daily lives, and where the nuanced interactions with brands shape our perceptions and experiences in profound ways.

Resources: Get in those spaces. See how other brands execute in the space. Pay attention to the economy and communities in the Unreal engine. Without the platforms, those communities can't exist.

Post-smartphone future: Scaman discussed "ambient computing"—where people don't even notice a device doing computing. It's in the background. Spatial Computing in every task will not be noticeable, yet it will improve people's lives. Spatial Computing will live in smart glasses, one's bathroom mirror, or even an implantable device.

BX: BX is the impression left on people after interaction with a brand. People don't even need to be customers of a brand to have a positive or negative BX. In modern culture, brands are held to higher standards. For example, the BX could include the diversity of panel speakers at a conference. Or the sustainability of a fashion brand. The authenticity of a brand and its values is a part of the BX. Brands can use AI and Spatial Computing to create a positive impact on their brand's image and experience.

In this chapter, we explored how AI-driven Spatial Computing will impact CX, UX, and EX, and how we are on the verge of a transition into B2R2C. We explored how the way we experience and engage with each other, with goods, with work, and with technology will evolve and impact both our employees and our customers.

In the next chapter, we will dive deeper into strategy and implementation and venture into the future of AI-driven Spatial Computing.

PART 3

Strategy, Implementation, and the Future

CHAPTER 7

Risks, Challenges, and Ethical Considerations

The integration of Spatial Computing and AI marks a watershed moment in the trajectory of technological evolution. This fusion is not merely an incremental advancement, but a transformative leap, ushering in a new era where digital and physical realms intersect with unprecedented precision and intelligence. The convergence of Spatial Computing—a technology that enables computers to perceive, analyze, and interact with the physical world—and AI, known for its ability to learn, adapt, and make decisions, is unlocking possibilities that were once confined to the realm of science fiction.

Spatial Computing, by its very nature, extends the reach of computation into the 3D space we inhabit. It allows computers and digital systems to understand and manipulate the spatial properties and dynamics of objects, environments, and human interactions within those spaces. When infused with AI, these systems are not just passively mapping and interacting with space, but are also actively learning from it, adapting to it, and potentially predicting or influencing future spatial dynamics.

The implications of this integration are far-reaching and multifaceted. In the world of AR/VR, it is revolutionizing the way we experience and interact with both virtual and augmented realities, creating immersive experiences that blur the lines between the digital and the physical. In the automotive industry, the combination is at the heart of developing autonomous vehicles that can safely navigate complex environments. Urban planning and management are also being transformed, as smart city initiatives leverage these technologies to enhance efficiency, sustainability, and quality of urban life.

Yet, while the benefits are profound, the integration of Spatial Computing and AI also brings forth a spectrum of risks, challenges, and ethical considerations that demand careful attention. As these technologies become more ingrained in our daily lives, their impact stretches beyond mere functionality and convenience, touching on deeper issues of privacy, security, ethics, and societal norms. Ensuring the responsible development and deployment of these technologies is not just a technical challenge, but also a moral imperative.

In the following discussion, we delve into these aspects in detail, examining the multifaceted implications of this technological confluence. From privacy concerns and ethical challenges to legal, regulatory, and societal impacts, we aim to provide a comprehensive overview of the considerations that need to be at the forefront as we navigate this exciting, yet complex, technological frontier.

Risks

The integration of Spatial Computing and AI heralds a new era of technological advancement, but it also brings with it a host of risks that need to be carefully understood and managed. These risks span various domains, from privacy and security concerns to unintended consequences and environmental impacts.

Data Privacy and Personal Information Security

The risks associated with data privacy and personal information security in the context of Spatial Computing and AI are both profound and pervasive. As these systems inherently collect and process extensive data about their environments, including potentially private spaces, the scope for privacy invasion is significant. This data, often detailed and comprehensive, can inadvertently reveal intimate aspects of an individual's life, such as their daily routines, preferences, and even behavioral patterns. The implications for personal privacy are immense, as this could lead to scenarios where individuals are unknowingly tracked or profiled based on their spatial data.

Moreover, the susceptibility of these systems to cyberattacks poses a serious threat to personal information security. Hackers targeting these systems could gain access to sensitive personal data, leading to risks like identity theft, financial fraud, and personal safety concerns. The nature of the data involved—often granular and encompassing—makes such breaches particularly invasive.

Unauthorized surveillance is another critical risk in this domain. The potential for Spatial Computing and AI technologies to be used for covert monitoring of individuals raises significant ethical and legal concerns. Such surveillance, whether by government entities, corporations, or malicious actors, could lead to a systematic erosion of privacy rights and civil liberties. The issue is exacerbated by the often opaque nature of these technologies, where individuals may not be aware of or able to consent to the extent of monitoring and data collection taking place.

Security Vulnerabilities

Security vulnerabilities in Spatial Computing and AI systems represent a significant and multifaceted risk. The inherent complexity and interconnectedness of these systems make them particularly susceptible to cyber threats. Hackers exploiting these vulnerabilities could manipulate spatial data, leading to a range of harmful outcomes. For example, in the context of autonomous vehicles, a security breach could result in the manipulation of navigational data, posing serious safety risks to passengers and pedestrians. In AR applications, compromised data could lead to the creation of misleading or harmful virtual elements in the user's environment.

The risk extends beyond individual applications to broader systems. As urban infrastructure and services increasingly rely on Spatial Computing and AI—for instance, in traffic management, public safety monitoring, and utility services—security vulnerabilities in these systems could have widespread and disruptive consequences. A cyberattack on a city's smart infrastructure could paralyze essential services, impacting everything from emergency response capabilities to the daily commute of millions.

Furthermore, the growing societal dependence on these technologies amplifies the impact of potential security failures. As Spatial Computing and AI become integral to more aspects of daily life and critical infrastructure, the fallout from system breaches or malfunctions becomes more severe. This not only raises concerns about immediate safety and service disruptions, but also about the longer-term resilience and security of our increasingly tech-dependent societies.

Addressing the risks associated with data privacy, personal information security, and security vulnerabilities in Spatial Computing and AI systems is essential. These concerns require a multifaceted approach, encompassing robust cybersecurity measures, clear privacy regulations, and heightened public awareness. Ensuring the ethical development and deployment of these technologies is crucial to safeguarding personal privacy and the security of our digital and physical environments.

Unintended Consequences and Decision-Making Flaws

The risks of unintended consequences and decision-making flaws in AI systems, especially when integrated with Spatial Computing, are significant and multifaceted. One of the primary concerns is the potential for AI algorithms to misinterpret spatial data, which can lead to incorrect and sometimes dangerous decisions. In healthcare, for instance, an AI system that misinterprets data in a medical imaging context could lead to misdiagnosis or inappropriate treatment plans. In transportation, an erroneous interpretation of spatial data by an autonomous vehicle's AI could result in navigation errors, or in the worst case, accidents that endanger human lives.

The unpredictability of AI systems, particularly those employing complex ML models, adds another layer of risk. These systems, while powerful in their data processing and pattern recognition capabilities, can sometimes produce results that are not fully understood by their human operators. This unpredictability is a concern in dynamic, real-world environments where decisions need to be made quickly and accurately. For example, an AI system managing urban traffic flow might react in unforeseen ways to unusual traffic patterns, potentially causing congestion or accidents.

Socio-Technical System Disruptions

The integration of Spatial Computing and AI poses significant risks to existing socio-technical systems. As these technologies become more prevalent, they have the potential to disrupt traditional job markets and skill sets. Automation driven by AI can lead to the displacement of jobs, especially in sectors like manufacturing, logistics, and even some aspects of professional services. This shift could result in significant socio-economic challenges, including increased unemployment and the need for large-scale retraining programs.

Furthermore, the growing reliance on these technologies could lead to societal vulnerabilities. In the event of technological failures or outages, societies that are heavily dependent on these systems might face severe disruptions. For instance, a major failure in a smart city's infrastructure, such as its power grid or communication networks, could lead to widespread chaos, affecting everything from emergency services to everyday conveniences.

Ethical Misuse and Abuse of Technology

The ethical misuse and potential abuse of Spatial Computing and AI technologies present profound risks. These technologies could be employed in ways that infringe on individual rights and privacy, such as through unauthorized mass surveillance. The use of AI in creating AR experiences could also lead to ethical dilemmas, particularly if these experiences are used to deceive or manipulate users.

Moreover, the application of these technologies in military and defense contexts raises significant ethical concerns. The development of autonomous weapons systems, for example, poses questions about the ethics of delegating life-and-death decisions to machines. These concerns extend to the broader implications of using AI in warfare, including issues of accountability, civilian safety, and the potential for escalation in armed conflicts.

Environmental Impact

The environmental impact of Spatial Computing and AI technologies is an increasingly pressing concern. The energy consumption required to power these advanced systems is significant, contributing to the broader issue of carbon emissions and climate change. Data centers, which are central to the functioning of these technologies, consume vast amounts of energy, raising questions about the sustainability of current technological practices.

Additionally, the rapid evolution of these technologies can contribute to the problem of electronic waste. As new devices and systems are developed, older models become obsolete, often ending up as electronic waste. This not only adds to the growing problem of waste management, but also raises concerns about the sustainable and ethical sourcing of materials used in these technologies. The need for responsible production, consumption, and disposal practices is thus a crucial aspect of managing the environmental impact of Spatial Computing and AI.

The integration of Spatial Computing and AI, while offering immense potential, is accompanied by a range of risks that need to be thoughtfully addressed. These include concerns over privacy, security, unintended consequences, sociotechnical disruptions, ethical misuse, and environmental impacts. Addressing these risks requires a comprehensive approach that includes technological solutions, ethical guidelines, regulatory frameworks, and active engagement with societal implications.

Challenges

The convergence of Spatial Computing and AI represents a significant milestone in technological advancement, bringing forth new opportunities and innovations. However, this integration also introduces a wide array of challenges, each as intricate and diverse as the technologies themselves. These challenges span from technical complexities to operational difficulties, as well as broader developmental and societal issues, all requiring tailored strategies for effective resolution.

At the core of these challenges is the task of successfully integrating sophisticated AI algorithms with the dynamic and voluminous data produced by Spatial Computing systems. This necessitates not only a profound understanding of both domains, but also a capacity to anticipate and address the numerous interactions between these advanced technologies. Operationally, the challenges involve implementing and managing these systems in real-world environments, where unpredictability is commonplace and the implications of failure can be significant.

Beyond the technical and operational aspects, the broader developmental challenges involve considering the impact of these technologies on broader societal structures. This includes assessing potential effects on employment, privacy, ethical usage, and the overall long-term changes these technologies may bring about in various sectors of society. Addressing these challenges demands a multidisciplinary approach that goes beyond technological expertise to include insights from social, ethical, and economic perspectives.

Overall, the challenges associated with the integration of Spatial Computing and AI are as stimulating as they are complex. They represent a crucial aspect of our ongoing technological journey, necessitating collaborative efforts from developers, researchers, policymakers, and the broader society. As we continue to explore and refine the synergy between these technologies, addressing these challenges will be essential to harness their collective potential and ensure a positive and meaningful impact on our world.

Complexity of Integration

The challenge of integrating AI with Spatial Computing systems is a task marked by its complexity and technical demands. This integration requires a sophisticated blend of software and hardware engineering to ensure that the advanced AI algorithms can effectively interpret and interact with the rich, three-dimensional data generated by Spatial Computing. Achieving this harmony is not just about making two technologies work together; it involves creating a seamless, efficient, and reliable interplay between them.

One of the key aspects of this challenge is the need for real-time data processing. In applications such as interactive AR/VR and autonomous vehicles, there is no room for latency. The AI must process spatial data in real time, making immediate decisions based on constantly changing environmental inputs. This requires not only powerful computing capabilities, but also algorithms that are optimized for speed and efficiency. The intricacy of this task is heightened by the diverse range of environments and scenarios in which these systems must operate, from the controlled settings of AR/VR to the unpredictable nature of real-world driving.

Reliability and Accuracy Demands

Ensuring high reliability and accuracy in AI's interpretation of spatial data is another significant challenge. Spatial environments are inherently complex and dynamic, filled with unpredictable elements that AI systems must accurately interpret and respond to. In fields where precision is critical, such as medical AR applications or autonomous driving, the stakes are incredibly high. An error in data interpretation or decision-making could have serious, even life-threatening, consequences.

Developing AI systems that can consistently deliver this level of accuracy involves overcoming numerous hurdles. These include ensuring the AI is trained on diverse and comprehensive data sets to understand the nuances of different spatial environments. It also involves developing robust algorithms capable of adapting to new and unforeseen scenarios while maintaining a high level of accuracy. This challenge is further compounded by the need to ensure that these systems are resilient to various forms of data degradation or interference that could impact their decision-making.

Real-Time Data Processing

The requirement for real-time, or near-instantaneous, data processing in Spatial Computing is a formidable challenge. AI systems in this context are expected to process and analyze complex spatial data rapidly to make timely and accurate decisions. Given the computational intensity of many AI processes, this poses a significant technical hurdle.

Balancing the need for swift data processing with the complexity and depth of analysis required is a delicate act. It involves optimizing algorithms for speed without sacrificing the depth of analysis. Moreover, these systems often need to operate in environments where network connectivity may be variable, adding another layer of complexity to real-time data processing.

The challenge is also in ensuring that these systems can handle the sheer volume of data typical in Spatial Computing applications. For instance, in an autonomous vehicle, the AI must process data from various sensors (like LiDAR, cameras, and GPS) in real time, synthesizing this information to make split-second decisions. Achieving this level of performance consistently and reliably is a key challenge in the successful integration of AI with Spatial Computing.

Scalability and Flexibility

The scalability and flexibility of Spatial Computing and AI technologies pose a considerable challenge in their development and deployment. As these technologies are increasingly applied in various sectors, they must be designed to handle escalating amounts of data and growing complexities. This scalability is crucial, especially in rapidly evolving domains such as smart cities and AR/VR, where the volume and variety of data can be immense.

Moreover, the flexibility of these systems is equally important. They need to be adaptable to a range of environments and use cases, capable of evolving alongside technological advancements and changing user needs. This flexibility involves not just scaling up in terms of data handling and processing capabilities, but also adapting to new forms of data, different operational contexts, and emerging user requirements. The challenge lies in designing systems that are both robust in their core functionalities and agile enough to evolve over time.

Designing User Interfaces and Experiences

Creating user interfaces and experiences for systems that integrate Spatial Computing with AI presents unique challenges. These interfaces must be intuitive and easy to navigate, ensuring that users can effectively interact with the technology regardless of their technical expertise. This is particularly crucial in making these advanced technologies accessible and user-friendly to a broad audience.

The challenge is compounded by the diverse nature of applications for these technologies. Designers must account for a wide range of use cases, from the immersive environments of AR/VR to the practical applications in smart city infrastructures or autonomous vehicles. Crafting experiences that are engaging, informative, and efficient across such a varied landscape requires a deep understanding of user psychology, ergonomic principles, and interactive design. It's a balancing act between harnessing the advanced capabilities of these technologies and presenting them in a manner that is approachable and meaningful to users.

Ensuring Interoperability and Standardization

Achieving interoperability among various Spatial Computing and AI systems is another significant challenge. For these technologies to function harmoniously and be widely adopted, they must be able to interact seamlessly with one another. This interoperability is essential for building a cohesive ecosystem of devices and applications that can work together effectively.

Developing and adhering to industry standards plays a critical role in this context. Standards ensure that systems from different manufacturers or developers can communicate and operate together without compatibility issues. The challenge lies in creating these standards in a rapidly evolving technological landscape and ensuring they are adopted universally. This requires collaboration among industry leaders, developers, and regulatory bodies to establish guidelines that are both forward-looking and adaptable to future advancements.

Data Management Complexity

The challenge of managing the vast volume and complexity of data associated with Spatial Computing and AI systems is immense and multifaceted. These systems generate, accumulate, and process an extraordinary amount of data, ranging from detailed environmental scans to user interactions and behaviors. Effectively handling this data requires not only robust storage solutions, but also advanced strategies for data processing and analysis.

One key aspect of this challenge is ensuring efficiency in data management. Systems must be able to store and access large data sets rapidly and reliably, often in real-time or near-real-time scenarios. This necessitates the use of high-performance computing solutions and optimized databases capable of handling high-throughput data with minimal latency.

Another crucial aspect is the maintenance of system performance and reliability while managing this data. Systems must be resilient, capable of functioning effectively under varying loads and conditions. They must also be designed with fail-safe mechanisms to ensure continuous operation, even in the face of potential hardware or software failures.

Additionally, data privacy and security are paramount. As these systems often handle sensitive personal or proprietary information, robust security protocols must be in place to protect against unauthorized access and data breaches. This involves implementing advanced encryption methods, secure data transmission protocols, and rigorous access controls, along with ongoing monitoring and vulnerability assessments to guard against emerging cyber threats.

Navigating Ethical and Social Impacts

Addressing the societal and ethical implications of integrating Spatial Computing with AI is a profound and complex challenge that overlaps with broader ethical considerations. As these technologies become more ingrained in our daily lives, their influence on society becomes more significant and far-reaching. Developers, policymakers, and stakeholders are thus faced with the task of understanding and navigating these impacts.

One of the primary concerns in this area is privacy. The capability of these technologies to collect and analyze detailed spatial and personal data raises significant privacy issues. Ensuring that this data is used ethically and responsibly, with respect for individual privacy rights, is a crucial challenge.

Personal autonomy is another key consideration. As decision-making processes become increasingly automated and influenced by AI, there is a risk of diminishing human agency and control. Ensuring that these technologies enhance rather than undermine personal autonomy is essential.

The potential impacts on employment also warrant careful consideration. As Spatial Computing and AI technologies automate more tasks and
processes, there is a risk of job displacement and the widening of skills gaps.
Addressing these issues requires proactive strategies, such as workforce
retraining programs and the development of new job roles that complement
these technologies.

In essence, the challenges associated with merging Spatial Computing
and AI span technical, operational, and societal realms. Addressing these
challenges is a collective endeavor, necessitating the collaboration of technologists, designers, policymakers, and industry experts. It involves not
only solving complex technical problems, but also considering UX, compatibility, adaptability, and the wider ethical and societal ramifications of these
advanced technologies.

Ethical Considerations

The integration of Spatial Computing and AI technologies represents a significant advancement in the field of technology, introducing powerful capabilities with far-reaching implications. However, this integration also raises
a complex array of ethical considerations that are critical to address for the
responsible development and deployment of these technologies. These ethical
issues are not just multifaceted, but also deeply interconnected, encompassing aspects such as privacy, autonomy, fairness, societal impact, and beyond.
They present not only technical challenges, but also moral and philosophical
questions about how these technologies should be utilized and governed.

Understanding and addressing these ethical considerations is not merely
a compliance or regulatory issue; it is a fundamental aspect of ensuring that
the development and application of Spatial Computing and AI are aligned
with societal values and human rights principles. The ethical dimensions of
these technologies touch on the very essence of privacy rights, the nature of
human decision-making, the fairness of automated systems, and the broader
societal consequences of technological advancements.

The task of navigating these ethical challenges is as crucial as it is complex. It requires a thoughtful and proactive approach, one that considers the
long-term implications of these technologies on individuals, communities,
and society as a whole. This involves not only the technologists and developers who are at the forefront of creating these systems, but also a broader
coalition of stakeholders, including ethicists, policymakers, social scientists,
and the public. Together, these groups must engage in ongoing dialogue and
collaboration to ensure that the benefits of Spatial Computing and AI are realized in a way that is ethically sound, socially responsible, and conducive to the
betterment of humanity.

Privacy and Data Protection

We've already addressed this in the "Risks" section, but it should be noted here as well. A primary ethical concern with the integration of Spatial Computing and AI is the protection of individual privacy. These technologies have the capability to collect, process, and analyze vast amounts of data, some of which can be extremely personal or sensitive. Ensuring that this data is collected and used in a manner that respects individual privacy rights is paramount. This includes implementing robust data protection measures, securing informed consent where necessary, and ensuring transparency in how data is used.

Autonomy and Human Agency

The integration of Spatial Computing and AI poses profound questions regarding human autonomy and agency. As AI algorithms become more sophisticated and integral to decision-making processes, there is a growing concern about the potential overshadowing of human judgment and choice. This concern is particularly acute in critical areas, such as healthcare, where AI might assist in diagnostic processes; law enforcement, where it could influence decision-making in public safety; and employment, where it may automate job roles.

The central ethical challenge lies in ensuring that these technologies function as aids that enhance human decision-making, rather than as replacements that diminish or supplant it. In healthcare, for instance, while AI can provide valuable insights and analyses, the final clinical decisions should ideally incorporate the practitioner's expertise and understanding of the patient's unique context. Similarly, in law enforcement, while AI can help in predictive analytics, it is crucial that final decisions are tempered by human discretion and an understanding of social complexities.

Maintaining a balance between automated decision-making and human oversight is essential to preserve individual autonomy. This involves designing systems that support and enhance human decision-making, rather than making decisions on behalf of individuals. It also means establishing clear guidelines and boundaries for the role of AI in decision-making processes, ensuring that there is always room for human intervention, oversight, and accountability.

Fairness and Bias

Fairness and bias in AI algorithms are critical ethical considerations, especially pertinent in the context of Spatial Computing. AI systems, by their nature, learn from and reflect the data they are trained on. If this data contains biases, the AI's decisions and behaviors will likely perpetuate these biases. This risk is particularly concerning in sensitive applications like facial recognition, where biased algorithms can lead to unfair treatment of certain groups, or in predictive policing, where they could reinforce discriminatory practices.

To address these issues, it is essential to design and continuously evaluate AI algorithms for fairness and impartiality. This process involves not only using diverse and representative data sets in training, but also incorporating mechanisms to detect and correct biases that may emerge. Developers and data scientists need to be acutely aware of the origins of their data and the potential biases it may contain as well as the social and cultural contexts in which their algorithms will operate.

Moreover, there needs to be an ongoing dialogue and collaboration among technologists, ethicists, and representatives of diverse communities to ensure that these technologies are developed and deployed in a manner that is fair and equitable. Establishing frameworks and guidelines for ethical AI development, along with regular audits and assessments of AI systems, can help mitigate the risk of bias and ensure that these technologies are beneficial and fair to all segments of society.

Societal Impact

The integration of Spatial Computing and AI is poised to reshape various facets of society, impacting how we interact with our surroundings, conduct our professional duties, and communicate with one another. This technological transformation, while offering significant advancements, also introduces complex ethical and societal challenges that necessitate thorough consideration and strategic management.

Transformation of interaction and work: The way we interact with our environment and perform our work is fundamentally changing due to the integration of Spatial Computing and AI. In fields like architecture and urban planning, these technologies enable more immersive and accurate design experiences. In healthcare, they offer new dimensions in patient care and diagnostics. However, these advancements also bring potential disruptions. For instance, in sectors where AI can automate complex tasks, there's a looming challenge of redefining human roles and skills. The workforce may need to adapt to new paradigms where AI complements human skills, necessitating significant shifts in education and training.

Job displacement and workforce transformation: One of the more immediate concerns is the potential for job displacement due to automation. As AI and Spatial Computing automate routine and even complex tasks, certain job roles may become obsolete. This shift calls for a proactive approach to workforce development, focusing on retraining and upskilling programs. Governments, educational institutions, and industries need to collaborate to prepare the workforce for this transition, ensuring that individuals have the necessary skills to thrive in an AI-augmented job market.

Shifts in social dynamics: The integration of these technologies also influences social dynamics. The way people interact with each other and with technology itself is evolving. For example, AR and VR offer new ways of social interaction and entertainment, but they also raise questions about the nature of social relationships and the psychological impacts of prolonged immersion in virtual environments.

Widening digital divide: As Spatial Computing and AI technologies advance, there's a risk of exacerbating the digital divide. Access to cutting-edge technology often correlates with socio-economic status, potentially leaving behind those in lower-income groups or in less developed regions. This divide not only pertains to access to technology, but also to the skills and knowledge necessary to utilize these advancements effectively. Bridging this divide is essential to prevent the creation of a society segregated by technological access and proficiency.

Cultural considerations: The societal impact of these technologies extends to the cultural realm. Different cultures may have varying perspectives on the integration of technology into daily life, and navigating these differences is crucial to ensure a respectful and inclusive approach.

Ethical Use in Sensitive Applications

The ethical implications of using Spatial Computing and AI in sensitive applications present a particularly challenging and contentious area of concern. Applications, such as surveillance, law enforcement, and military operations, where these technologies can have direct and significant impacts on individual rights and societal norms, are under intense scrutiny. The potential for misuse or abuse of these technologies in such contexts raises profound ethical dilemmas, necessitating stringent oversight and ethical governance.

Surveillance: The use of Spatial Computing and AI in surveillance has the potential to significantly enhance public safety and security. However, it also raises critical privacy concerns. The ability of these systems to monitor, track, and analyze individuals and groups can lead to invasive privacy breaches and the erosion of civil liberties. It is essential to establish clear boundaries and regulations governing the use of these technologies in surveillance to protect individual privacy rights and prevent the creation of a surveillance state.

Law enforcement: In law enforcement, these technologies can aid in crime prevention and investigation. However, their use must be balanced against the risk of infringing on personal freedoms and rights. Issues, such as bias in facial recognition software, which can lead to wrongful identification and profiling, need to be carefully addressed. Ensuring transparency in how these technologies are used and incorporating checks and balances to prevent abuse are crucial in maintaining public trust and upholding justice.

Military applications: The deployment of Spatial Computing and AI in military applications, such as autonomous weapons systems, raises critical ethical questions about the nature of warfare and the role of human oversight in combat decisions. The prospect of machines making life-or-death decisions autonomously is a source of significant ethical and philosophical debate. International laws and ethical standards governing the use of such technologies in military contexts must be established and rigorously enforced to prevent unethical use and to maintain human control over lethal decision-making.

Ensuring the ethical use of Spatial Computing and AI in these sensitive applications is a multifaceted challenge. It requires the development of comprehensive ethical guidelines, strict regulatory frameworks, and robust oversight mechanisms. This task demands the collaboration of a wide array of stakeholders, including technologists, ethicists, policymakers, law enforcement authorities, military officials, and the public. Navigating these ethical challenges is critical to ensuring that the deployment and application of these technologies align with fundamental societal values, human rights, and ethical principles. Only through such a concerted and transparent effort can the benefits of Spatial Computing and AI be harnessed in a manner that is both socially responsible and ethically sound.

Synopsis

The integration of Spatial Computing and AI presents unprecedented opportunities and substantial responsibilities. Our exploration into the array of risks, challenges, and ethical considerations associated with this technological convergence reveals a complex and critical path that must be navigated with precision and foresight.

The risks associated with this integration extend beyond mere technical hurdles, entering the area of societal impact. From the potential for AI algorithms to misinterpret spatial data, leading to flawed decision-making, to the disruption of socio-technical systems potentially altering job landscapes and societal norms, the implications are vast. The possibility of these technologies being used unethically, especially in areas like surveillance and defense, raises significant moral questions. Furthermore, the environmental footprint of these technologies, encompassing both energy consumption and electronic waste, underscores the need for environmentally conscious development strategies.

The challenges in seamlessly integrating Spatial Computing with AI are as intricate as the technologies themselves. This includes the daunting task of harmonizing advanced AI algorithms with the constantly evolving nature of spatial data. Ensuring the reliability and precision of these systems, particularly in critical areas such as healthcare and autonomous transportation, adds another layer of complexity. Additionally, the demands for real-time data processing, scalability, and adaptability in these systems further amplify the complexity of their development and implementation.

Within this landscape of risks and challenges, ethical considerations emerge as a crucial compass, guiding the direction of technological advancement toward alignment with societal values and ethical norms. Safeguarding privacy and data security in an era where technology can intrude into private spaces is of utmost importance. Upholding human autonomy in the face of automated decision-making, and ensuring the absence of bias in AI algorithms, are key to maintaining societal trust and fairness. Addressing the wider societal impacts, such as potential job shifts and the widening digital divide, necessitates a comprehensive approach that considers the human and social facets alongside technological progress.

Ultimately, the fusion of Spatial Computing and AI is not merely a technological quest, but a journey that encompasses societal implications, calling for collaborative efforts from a diverse array of stakeholders including technologists, ethicists, policymakers, and the public. Navigating this journey with careful consideration, responsibility, and an acute understanding of the deep-seated implications these technologies have on our future is imperative. The decisions and actions taken in response to these risks, challenges, and ethical considerations will not only define the future of technological evolution, but also shape the social and moral landscape of our times.

CHAPTER 8

Your Spatial Computing and AI Roadmap: From Strategy to Implementation and Beyond

With Spatial Computing and AI, organizations are navigating a complex journey. This journey involves harnessing the potential of these advanced technologies to foster innovation, enhance efficiency, and gain a competitive edge. This chapter serves as an essential guide, offering a structured and comprehensive pathway for integrating these technologies into your organization's operational and strategic frameworks.

The convergence of Spatial Computing and AI represents a significant shift in the technological paradigm. Embarking on this integration journey necessitates a strategic roadmap. Such a roadmap is not merely a sequence of steps, but a holistic plan that aligns with the organization's overarching goals and capabilities. It requires meticulous planning, efficient resource allocation, and thoughtful management to ensure successful implementation and integration.

This roadmap encompasses several critical phases. It begins with strategic planning, highlighting the need to align technological integration with the organization's business objectives and readiness. Following this, the focus shifts to the selection and integration of the right technologies, ensuring they seamlessly blend into existing systems and processes.

The implementation phase is detailed and critical, involving steps, such as setting up the necessary infrastructure, training employees, and deploying the technology effectively. However, the journey does not end with implementation. Ongoing monitoring and optimization are essential to ensure that the technologies continue to serve the intended purpose effectively.

Moreover, the roadmap addresses vital aspects, such as compliance and ethics, particularly crucial in AI applications. It emphasizes the importance of adhering to legal standards and maintaining ethical practices in technology deployment. Another key aspect covered is risk management, which involves identifying potential risks and developing strategies to mitigate them effectively.

Effective reporting and communication throughout the process are crucial for success. Clear communication channels and regular progress reports ensure that all stakeholders are aligned and informed.

Last, the roadmap prepares organizations for future trends and adaptation. In a field as rapidly evolving as Spatial Computing and AI, staying ahead means being prepared to adapt and evolve with emerging technologies and market shifts. This forward-thinking approach is essential for long-term success and sustainability in the ever-evolving landscape of Spatial Computing and AI. We begin here with strategic planning.

Strategic Planning

Strategic planning for Spatial Computing and AI within organizations involves a tailored approach that focuses on integrating these advanced technologies into the broader business strategy. Given the specialized nature of Spatial Computing and AI technologies, this process requires a deep understanding of the technological landscape as well as the organization's capabilities and goals.

Understanding the potential of Spatial Computing and AI: The first step in strategic planning is to comprehend the potential and implications of the combination of Spatial Computing and AI technologies. This book's aim is to do that very thing. Understanding how these technologies can be leveraged to create value is fundamental to effective strategic planning.

Aligning technology with business objectives: The core of the strategic planning process is aligning the capabilities of the technologies with the organization's business objectives. This involves identifying areas where these technologies can enhance operational efficiency, drive innovation, improve customer experiences, or create new business models. The key is to integrate these technologies in a way that supports the overall vision and mission of the organization.

Assessing organizational readiness: A critical aspect of the strategic planning process is assessing the organization's readiness to adopt the combination of Spatial Computing and AI. This assessment should consider the existing technological infrastructure, the skill level of the workforce, the organizational culture, and the current level of digital transformation within the organization.

Developing a roadmap: Developing a strategic roadmap is essential for the successful implementation of Spatial Computing and AI initiatives. This roadmap should outline the key milestones, timelines, and resource allocation required to achieve the strategic objectives. It should also include plans for scaling up initiatives and integrating them across different departments and functions within the organization.

Identifying and mitigating risks: Integrating Spatial Computing and AI into business operations comes with its set of risks, including technological, regulatory, ethical, and operational risks. Strategic planning must involve identifying these risks and developing mitigation strategies. This includes ensuring compliance with data protection regulations, addressing ethical concerns related to AI, and managing the impact on the workforce.

Investing in talent and training: The successful implementation of Spatial Computing and AI strategies requires investing in the right talent and training. Organizations may need to hire new talent with specialized skills in these areas or provide training to existing employees. Developing a culture of continuous learning and innovation is also crucial for keeping pace with technological advancements.

Fostering partnerships and collaborations: Strategic planning should also consider the potential for partnerships and collaborations. Engaging with technology providers, research institutions, and other organizations can provide access to specialized knowledge, emerging technologies, and new market opportunities. These collaborations can be vital for staying at the forefront of technological innovation.

Continual monitoring and adaptation: The field of Spatial Computing and AI is rapidly evolving. Therefore, strategic plans should not be static, but require continual monitoring and adaptation. This involves staying abreast of technological developments, market trends, changing customer needs, and being ready to adjust strategies accordingly.

In essence, strategic planning in organizations is a dynamic and complex process. It requires a clear understanding of these cutting-edge technologies, their alignment with business objectives, and an adaptable approach to integration and implementation. By thoroughly assessing organizational readiness, developing a comprehensive roadmap, investing in talent, and fostering collaborations, organizations can harness the transformative potential of Spatial Computing and AI, positioning themselves for long-term success and innovation.

Technology Selection and Integration

Technology selection and integration is a critical process for any organization looking to stay competitive and efficient in today's fast-paced digital environment. This process involves several key stages, from assessing needs and evaluating options to implementing and managing the selected technologies.

Technology selection and integration: Choosing and integrating the right Spatial Computing and AI technologies within an organization is a nuanced process. It involves identifying technologies that not only align with the company's specific needs, but also enhance its capabilities in these advanced fields.

Assessing specific needs: The process begins with a thorough assessment of what the organization aims to achieve through Spatial Computing and AI. This requires a clear understanding of the problems these technologies can solve and the areas where they can add the most value, such as operational efficiency, customer engagement, or product innovation.

Exploring technological options: With a clear understanding of the organization's needs, the next step is to explore the available technological solutions. This involves examining various options in Spatial Computing and AI, assessing their capabilities, scalability, and how well they integrate with existing systems. The goal is to find technologies that are not only advanced, but also a good fit for the organization's current and future needs.

Conducting cost-benefit analysis: A critical component of the selection process is conducting a cost-benefit analysis. This helps in comparing the financial investment required for different technologies against their potential benefits. The analysis should consider both immediate costs and long-term operational expenses against expected improvements in efficiency, revenue generation, or customer satisfaction.

Pilot testing and feedback: Before fully integrating a new technology, pilot testing with a small group or department is advisable. This allows you to gather real-world data on the technology's performance and its impact on your operations. Feedback from users during this phase is crucial for understanding any issues or resistance, and for making necessary adjustments.

Integration planning: Integration planning involves developing a detailed strategy for how the new technology will be incorporated into your existing systems and processes. This includes technical integration, such as ensuring compatibility with current hardware and software, and operational integration, such as modifying workflows and processes to accommodate the new technology.

Training and support: Training and support are essential for successful technology integration. Employees need to be trained not only on how to use the new technology, but also on how it changes or improves their workflows. Adequate support should be available to address any issues or questions that arise during and after the integration process.

Monitoring and continuous improvement: After integration, continuous monitoring is essential to evaluate the technology's performance and impact. This involves measuring success against predefined metrics and making adjustments as needed. Continuous improvement is crucial to ensure that the technology remains effective and relevant.

Managing change: Integrating new technology often requires significant changes in the organization. Effective change management strategies are needed to help employees adapt to these changes. This includes clear communication about the reasons for the technology adoption, the benefits it brings, and how it affects individual roles and responsibilities.

Future updates and scalability: Finally, it's important to consider the future scalability and upgradability of the technology. As your organization grows and evolves, your technology needs may change. Selecting technologies that can scale and adapt to future requirements is essential for long-term success.

Selecting and integrating Spatial Computing and AI technologies into an organization is a multifaceted process. It requires careful consideration of the organization's needs, a detailed evaluation of technological options, and strategic planning for integration and adoption. With the right approach, organizations can successfully harness the potential of these advanced technologies, leading to significant improvements in innovation, efficiency, and competitiveness.

Implementation

The implementation of Spatial Computing and AI technologies in an organization encompasses a series of strategic steps, ensuring that these advanced tools are integrated effectively and contribute meaningfully to the organization's objectives.

Developing a comprehensive implementation plan: A well-defined implementation plan is critical. This plan should detail the steps, timelines, resources, and specific goals associated with the deployment of Spatial Computing and AI technologies. It needs to address technical aspects, such as software and hardware installation, integration with existing systems, and data migration as well as operational aspects, including process changes and workforce adaptation.

Forming a specialized implementation team: For effective implementation, it's advisable to form a team dedicated to overseeing the process. This team should ideally comprise individuals with technical expertise in Spatial Computing and AI, along with members who understand the organization's operational dynamics. Their role is to coordinate all activities, from technical deployment to user training.

Preparing infrastructure and systems: A critical phase in the implementation involves preparing the existing infrastructure and systems to support new technologies. Upgrades to hardware, modifications to existing software systems, and enhancements to network capabilities might be necessary to ensure compatibility and optimal performance of the new technologies.

Conducting training and providing support: Effective training programs are essential for staff to adapt to the new technologies. Training should be comprehensive, covering not only the technical aspects of the new tools, but also how they modify existing workflows. Ongoing support is crucial to resolve any operational issues post-implementation.

Data management and integration: If the new technologies involve data processing or management, proper data migration and integration are key. Ensuring that data is transferred accurately and securely to new systems, and that these systems are seamlessly integrated with existing databases, is crucial for maintaining data integrity and operational continuity.

Testing and quality assurance: Prior to a full-scale rollout, rigorous testing is necessary. This includes checking the functionality of the technologies, their compatibility with existing systems, and user acceptance. It's important to identify and resolve any issues in this phase to ensure smooth operation post-deployment.

Implementing in phases: A phased approach to implementation can be advantageous. It allows for the gradual introduction of the technology, enabling adjustments based on initial feedback and minimizing disruption. This approach can also help in managing the change more effectively across the organization.

Monitoring and feedback loop: After implementation, ongoing monitoring is crucial to track the performance and impact of the new technologies.

Establishing a feedback loop with users is important to gather insights on practical challenges and areas for improvement.

Overall, implementing Spatial Computing and AI in an organization is a complex process that extends beyond the mere installation of technology. It involves strategic planning, infrastructure preparation, effective training, and change management, all aimed at seamlessly integrating these advanced technologies into the organizational fabric. By carefully navigating these steps, organizations can unlock the full potential of Spatial Computing and AI, driving innovation and efficiency.

Monitoring and Optimization

Monitoring and optimization are critical stages in the lifecycle of implementing Spatial Computing and AI technologies in an organization. These processes ensure that the deployed technologies not only function as intended, but also continually improve and align with evolving organizational goals and market dynamics.

Establishing monitoring mechanisms: The first step is to establish robust monitoring mechanisms. This involves setting up systems to track the performance and usage of Spatial Computing and AI applications. Key Performance Indicators (KPIs) should be defined, aligning with the objectives set during the implementation phase. These KPIs could include metrics like system uptime, user engagement levels, error rates, and the accuracy of AI outputs.

Data analytics for performance insights: Utilizing data analytics is essential in monitoring. By analyzing usage data, error reports, and user feedback, organizations can gain valuable insights into how the technologies are performing. This analysis can reveal patterns and trends that help identify areas for improvement.

User feedback integration: User feedback is a vital component of the optimization process. Regularly collecting and analyzing feedback from employees and customers who interact with the Spatial Computing and AI systems can provide practical insights into UX and system effectiveness. This feedback can guide adjustments and enhancements.

Continuous improvement culture: Fostering a culture of continuous improvement is crucial. Encouraging employees to share their experiences and suggestions can lead to innovative ideas for enhancing the technology. Regular review meetings and brainstorming sessions can be effective forums for discussing potential improvements.

Regular technology assessments: Conducting regular technology assessments helps in staying abreast of the latest developments in Spatial Computing and AI. These assessments can inform decisions about updating or upgrading systems to leverage newer, more advanced capabilities.

Performance tuning and issue resolution: Active performance tuning and timely issue resolution are key to maintaining optimal functioning. This involves regularly updating software, fine-tuning AI algorithms, and addressing any technical glitches swiftly to minimize downtime and enhance user satisfaction.

Scalability and future-proofing: Monitoring should also focus on scalability. As the organization grows and its needs evolve, the Spatial Computing and AI systems should be able to scale accordingly. This means planning for the future in areas such as increased capacity, expanding features, or integrating additional modules as required.

Compliance and ethical considerations: With technologies like AI, it's important to continuously monitor compliance with regulatory standards and ethical guidelines. This includes ensuring data privacy, avoiding bias in AI algorithms, and maintaining transparency in AI-driven decisions.

Training and skill development: Ongoing training and skill development for staff are important for optimization. As the technologies evolve, employees need to stay updated with the latest features and best practices. This not only enhances their efficiency, but also ensures that the organization fully leverages the capabilities of the technologies.

Monitoring and optimization in the context of Spatial Computing and AI are ongoing processes that play a crucial role in maximizing the return on investment in these technologies. By systematically tracking performance, integrating user feedback, staying updated with technological advancements, and continuously improving the systems, organizations can ensure that their Spatial Computing and AI initiatives remain effective, relevant, and aligned with their strategic objectives.

Compliance and Ethics

In the implementation of Spatial Computing and AI, compliance and ethics are paramount. These considerations ensure that the organization not only adheres to legal standards, but also upholds moral and ethical responsibilities, which are especially crucial given the transformative nature of these technologies.

Understanding legal regulations and standards: The first step is to gain a comprehensive understanding of the legal landscape surrounding Spatial Computing and AI. This involves being aware of data protection laws, privacy regulations, and any industry-specific standards that apply to the use of these technologies. Regulations such as the General Data Protection Regulation (GDPR) in the European Union, and others across different jurisdictions, often have specific provisions regarding data privacy and AI.

Ethical framework development: Developing an ethical framework is critical. This framework should guide how the organization develops and uses Spatial Computing and AI technologies. Key considerations include ensuring fairness, transparency, and accountability in AI algorithms, and addressing concerns like bias and discrimination.

Data privacy and security: With technologies that heavily rely on data, like AI and Spatial Computing, ensuring data privacy and security is essential. This involves implementing robust data encryption, access controls, and secure data storage practices. Regular audits and updates to security protocols are also crucial to protect sensitive information.

Transparency in AI systems: Maintaining transparency in AI systems is important for building trust and accountability. This means having clear policies on how AI algorithms make decisions and ensuring that users understand the extent and limitations of AI interventions. In some cases, it may also involve providing options for human oversight or intervention in AI-driven processes.

Employee training and awareness: Educating employees about the legal and ethical aspects of Spatial Computing and AI is necessary. This training should cover the responsible use of these technologies, awareness of potential ethical dilemmas, and procedures for reporting violations or concerns.

Regular compliance audits: Conducting regular compliance audits can help ensure that the organization remains in line with legal and ethical standards. These audits should assess both the technological aspects, such as data handling and AI algorithm fairness, and the operational aspects, such as user consent and privacy policies.

Engaging with ethical AI communities: Participation in broader discussions and communities focused on ethical AI can be beneficial. Engaging with industry groups, attending conferences, and collaborating on research can provide insights into best practices and emerging ethical considerations in the field.

Addressing bias in AI: Proactively addressing bias in AI algorithms is a key ethical concern. This involves not only technical measures to identify and mitigate bias in AI models, but also broader organizational efforts to promote diversity and inclusion in technology design and decision-making.

Continuous review and adaptation: Ethics and compliance in the field of Spatial Computing and AI are continuously evolving. Regularly reviewing and updating policies and practices in light of new developments, research findings, and changing legal requirements is essential to maintain ethical integrity.

Incorporating compliance and ethics into the implementation of Spatial Computing and AI is not just a legal imperative, but also a moral obligation. It involves a comprehensive approach that encompasses understanding legal standards, developing ethical frameworks, ensuring data privacy, maintaining transparency, and addressing biases. By prioritizing these aspects, organizations can responsibly harness the power of these advanced technologies while maintaining public trust and upholding ethical standards.

Risk Management

Managing risks associated with the implementation of Spatial Computing and AI is crucial for organizations. This process involves identifying potential risks, assessing their impact, and developing strategies to mitigate them. Effective risk management ensures that the organization can leverage these technologies while minimizing negative consequences.

Identifying potential risks: The first step in risk management is to identify potential risks associated with Spatial Computing and AI. These risks can range from technological challenges, such as system failures or compatibility issues, to ethical concerns like data privacy breaches and AI biases. It also includes operational risks like disruptions to existing workflows and resistance to change from employees.

Risk assessment and prioritization: Once risks are identified, the next step is to assess their likelihood and potential impact. This assessment helps in prioritizing risks, allowing organizations to focus on managing those that could have the most significant consequences. Factors to consider include the severity of the impact, the probability of occurrence, and the organization's preparedness to address the risk.

Developing mitigation strategies: For each identified risk, a mitigation strategy should be developed. This may involve technical solutions, such as enhancing cybersecurity measures to protect against data breaches, or operational strategies, like conducting thorough testing to ensure system compatibility. It also includes implementing policies and procedures to address ethical concerns, such as establishing guidelines for AI development to prevent biases.

Continuity and disaster recovery planning: Developing a robust continuity and disaster recovery plan is crucial, especially for technology-driven processes. This plan should outline steps to restore normal operations in the event of a system failure or cyberattack. It includes data backups, alternative operational procedures, and resources allocation for recovery efforts.

Monitoring and regular review: Risk management is an ongoing process. Continuous monitoring of the Spatial Computing and AI systems is necessary to identify new risks as they emerge. Regularly reviewing and updating the risk management plan ensures that it remains relevant and effective in the face of technological advancements and changing organizational needs.

Employee training and awareness: Training employees on risk awareness and management practices is essential. They should be educated about potential risks associated with Spatial Computing and AI, and how to respond effectively in case of issues. This training helps in building a risk-conscious culture within the organization.

Legal and regulatory compliance: Ensuring compliance with legal and regulatory requirements is a critical aspect of risk management. This involves staying informed about relevant laws and regulations related to Spatial Computing and AI, and regularly reviewing practices and policies to ensure compliance.

Ethical considerations: Ethical risks, particularly in AI implementations, need special attention. This involves establishing ethical guidelines for AI use, such as ensuring transparency in AI decision-making processes and actively working to eliminate biases in AI algorithms.

Engaging with experts and partners: Collaborating with external experts and technology partners can help in effectively managing risks. These collaborations can provide access to specialized knowledge, emerging best practices, and additional resources for risk mitigation.

Risk management in the implementation of Spatial Computing and AI requires a comprehensive approach that covers technological, operational, legal, and ethical aspects. By identifying and assessing risks, developing targeted mitigation strategies, and fostering a culture of risk awareness and preparedness, organizations can navigate the challenges associated with these advanced technologies and maximize their benefits while minimizing potential downsides.

Reporting and Communication

Effective reporting and communication are essential in the implementation and ongoing management of Spatial Computing and AI technologies in organizations. These processes ensure that all stakeholders are informed about the progress, challenges, and successes of these initiatives, fostering transparency and support.

Establishing clear communication channels: The first step is to establish clear and efficient communication channels. These channels should cater to different stakeholders, including management, technical teams, employees, and possibly external partners. The goal is to ensure that relevant information is accessible to all parties involved.

Regular progress reports: Regular progress reports are crucial for keeping stakeholders informed about the status of Spatial Computing and AI projects. These reports should include updates on implementation progress, milestones achieved, challenges encountered, and next steps. They should be tailored to the audience, with technical details for IT teams and high-level summaries for executive management.

Communicating successes and challenges: Openly communicating both successes and challenges is important. While it's essential to highlight achievements and positive outcomes, acknowledging and discussing challenges helps in building trust and encourages collaborative problem-solving.

Feedback mechanisms: Implementing effective feedback mechanisms allows stakeholders to share their insights, concerns, and suggestions. This could be through regular meetings, surveys, suggestion boxes, or digital platforms. Feedback is invaluable for continuous improvement and for addressing any issues that arise during implementation.

Training and awareness sessions: Conducting training sessions and awareness programs for employees is a key aspect of communication. These sessions should educate staff about the benefits and potential of Spatial Computing and AI, how these technologies will impact their work, and how they can engage with these new tools effectively.

Data-driven reporting: Utilizing data-driven insights in reporting can significantly enhance the understanding of how Spatial Computing and AI are impacting the organization. Metrics and analytics can provide a clear picture of usage patterns, system performance, and ROI, facilitating informed decision-making.

Crisis communication plan: Having a crisis communication plan in place is crucial. In the event of a significant issue or failure, a well-defined plan ensures that accurate information is communicated promptly to the right stakeholders, helping to manage the situation effectively and minimize negative impacts.

Transparency in AI decision-making: Maintaining transparency, especially in AI-driven decisions, is critical. This involves communicating how AI models make decisions, the data they use, and their limitations. Transparency helps in building trust and acceptance among users and stakeholders.

Legal and regulatory updates: Keeping stakeholders informed about legal and regulatory updates related to Spatial Computing and AI is important. As these technologies are rapidly evolving, staying compliant requires ongoing communication about changes in policies and regulations.

Effective reporting and communication are integral to the successful implementation and management of Spatial Computing and AI technologies in organizations. By establishing clear communication channels, regularly reporting progress, fostering open dialogue about challenges and successes, and maintaining transparency, organizations can ensure that all stakeholders are aligned and engaged throughout the process. This approach not only facilitates smoother implementation but also helps in maximizing the benefits of these advanced technologies.

Future Trends and Adaptation

Staying attuned to future trends and adapting accordingly is crucial for organizations leveraging Spatial Computing and AI. This proactive approach ensures that they remain at the forefront of technological advancements, continue to innovate, and maintain a competitive edge.

Continuous market and technology research: Ongoing research into market trends and technological advancements is fundamental. Keeping an eye on how Spatial Computing and AI are evolving in different industries allows organizations to anticipate changes and identify emerging opportunities. This research should include not only technological developments, but also shifts in consumer behavior and expectations.

Developing a forward-looking mindset: Cultivating a forward-looking mindset within the organization is key. Encouraging employees to think about future possibilities and potential applications of Spatial Computing and AI can lead to innovative ideas and approaches. Workshops, brainstorming sessions, and innovation labs can be effective in fostering this mindset.

Building flexible and scalable systems: Incorporating flexibility and scalability into the design of Spatial Computing and AI systems is essential. As the technologies and market conditions evolve, having systems that can adapt to new requirements or scale up to accommodate growth is crucial. This approach reduces the need for complete overhauls and allows for incremental improvements.

Piloting and experimenting with emerging technologies: Experimentation is a critical component of adaptation. Piloting new features, tools, or approaches within Spatial Computing and AI allows organizations to test their viability and effectiveness before full-scale implementation. These pilot projects can provide valuable insights and inform future strategies.

Upskilling and reskilling workforce: Investing in the continuous education of the workforce is necessary to keep up with technological advancements. Providing training programs in the latest Spatial Computing and AI technologies and methodologies ensures that employees have the skills required to leverage these tools effectively.

Collaboration and networking: Engaging in collaborations and networking with other organizations, technology providers, and research institutions can provide valuable insights into future trends. These collaborations can also offer opportunities to co-develop new solutions or adapt existing ones to changing market needs.

Agile and responsive strategy development: Maintaining an agile and responsive approach to strategy development is important. This means being ready to adjust strategic plans based on new information, technological breakthroughs, or shifts in the business environment. Regular strategy reviews and updates should be part of the organization's routine.

Monitoring regulatory and ethical developments: Staying updated on regulatory and ethical developments related to Spatial Computing and AI is crucial. As these technologies advance, so do the legal and ethical frameworks governing their use. Organizations must adapt their practices to remain compliant and uphold ethical standards.

Leveraging predictive analytics: Using predictive analytics can help in anticipating future trends. By analyzing data patterns and trends, organizations can make more informed decisions about where Spatial Computing and AI technologies are heading and how best to prepare for these changes.

Adapting to future trends in Spatial Computing and AI requires a multifaceted approach. It involves continuous research and development, fostering a culture of innovation and forward-thinking, building flexible systems, upskilling the workforce, and maintaining agile strategies. By staying informed and prepared for future developments, organizations can not only adapt to changes, but also drive innovation and growth in an ever-evolving technological landscape.

Sustainability and Responsible AI

Incorporating sustainability and responsible practices in the use of Spatial Computing and AI is increasingly important. As these technologies advance, organizations must ensure that their applications are not only effective and innovative, but also ethically sound and environmentally sustainable.

Prioritizing ethical AI development: Developing AI in an ethical manner is paramount. This involves designing AI systems that are fair, transparent, and accountable. Organizations should establish guidelines to prevent biases in AI algorithms, ensure data privacy, and make AI decision-making processes understandable to users. Creating AI that respects ethical norms and societal values is crucial for long-term success and public trust.

Environmental impact assessment: Assessing the environmental impact of Spatial Computing and AI technologies is vital. This includes evaluating the energy consumption of data centers that power AI computations, the lifecycle impact of hardware used in Spatial Computing, and the overall carbon footprint of these technologies. Efforts should be made to minimize environmental impact, such as using renewable energy sources and adopting energy-efficient hardware.

Promoting sustainable practices: Promoting sustainable practices within the organization and its use of technology is important. This could involve implementing green computing initiatives, encouraging sustainable usage patterns among users, and opting for environmentally friendly hardware and software solutions.

Responsible data management: Responsible data management is a key aspect of sustainable and responsible AI. This means ensuring that data is collected, used, and stored in ways that respect user privacy and comply with data protection regulations. It also involves being transparent about data collection practices and giving users control over their data.

Ongoing compliance with regulations: Maintaining ongoing compliance with legal and regulatory standards, especially those related to environmental sustainability and ethical AI, is essential. As these regulations evolve, organizations must adapt their practices accordingly to remain compliant.

Employee education and training: Educating employees about the importance of sustainability and responsible AI is crucial. Training programs should cover responsible data handling, ethical AI development, and sustainable technology practices. Creating awareness among employees helps in embedding these values into the organization's culture.

Collaboration and partnerships: Collaborating with other organizations, industry groups, and regulatory bodies can enhance efforts in sustainability and responsible AI. These collaborations can lead to the sharing of best practices, development of industry standards, and joint efforts in addressing sustainability challenges.

Monitoring and reporting: Regular monitoring and reporting on sustainability and responsible AI practices are important for transparency and accountability. This involves tracking progress against sustainability goals, assessing the ethical implications of AI systems, and reporting these findings to stakeholders.

Leveraging AI for sustainability: Interestingly, AI itself can be a powerful tool for promoting sustainability. AI can help in optimizing energy usage, reducing waste, and enhancing resource efficiency. Organizations should explore how AI can be used to further their sustainability goals.

Focusing on sustainability and responsible AI is essential for organizations employing Spatial Computing and AI. By prioritizing ethical AI development, assessing environmental impacts, promoting sustainable practices, and ensuring compliance with evolving standards, organizations can not only enhance their operational efficiency and innovation, but also contribute positively to society and the environment.

In conclusion, the journey of integrating Spatial Computing and AI into an organization is both challenging and rewarding. This chapter provides a thorough guide to navigating this journey. From laying the foundational strategies to selecting and integrating the right technologies, from careful implementation to continuous monitoring and optimization, each step is crucial in harnessing the full potential of these transformative technologies. The roadmap emphasizes the importance of ethical considerations, compliance, effective risk management, and clear communication, ensuring that the integration of these technologies is not only technically sound, but also socially responsible and aligned with organizational values. As technologies continue to evolve, this roadmap serves as a vital tool for organizations to adapt, innovate, and lead in the realm of Spatial Computing and AI, setting the stage for a future where technology and human ingenuity converge to create unprecedented possibilities.

CHAPTER 9

Tomorrow and the Next Decade: Looking Ahead at What the Future Holds

O
ur last chapter is a deep dive into the transformative impact of Spatial Computing and AI on our world. This exploration goes beyond predicting technological advancements, focusing instead on how these technologies will fundamentally alter our everyday lives, redefine societal norms, and address global challenges.

Envision a daily life deeply integrated with ubiquitous Spatial Computing. AR and VR technologies, evolving into more user-friendly forms, will become essential tools in activities ranging from navigation to education and entertainment. AI's advancements in spatial reasoning will enhance the interaction between AR and VR systems and the physical world, making these experiences more intuitive and intelligent.

This future includes the development of Mixed Reality ecosystems, creating immersive environments that seamlessly merge the physical and digital. These ecosystems will enable smooth transitions between AR and VR, enriching our perception and interaction with the world.

UXs will be transformed through hyper-personalization, driven by AI. These tailored AR and VR experiences will offer levels of engagement and immersion unprecedented in current technology. Enhancements in haptic feedback and sensory technologies, such as spatial audio and olfactory interfaces, will add depth to these immersive experiences.

The implications of AI-driven Spatial Computing in healthcare, education, and business are significant. Healthcare will see advances in telemedicine and personalized treatments; education will be revolutionized with realistic simulations: businesses will adopt these technologies for innovative design, training, and customer engagement.

However, the growth of these technologies necessitates responsible development. Ethical guidelines and regulatory compliance will ensure their responsible use, emphasizing inclusivity, privacy, and user consent. Enhanced collaboration and connectivity will emerge from cross-platform integration and the advancement of beyond 5G networks, enabling more dynamic, real-time experiences.

The societal and cultural impacts of AI-driven Spatial Computing will be vast, altering communication, socialization, and creative expression. Sustainability and environmental considerations will also come to the forefront, emphasizing the need for sustainable practices and assessing the ecological impact of the technology's infrastructure.

This era presents a unique mix of opportunities and challenges. AI and Spatial Computing have the potential to democratize technology, yet they also bring uncertainty and demand adaptability. Lifelong learning will be crucial for professionals across all fields.

This chapter aims to prepare you for this imminent future, challenging you to reconsider your role and leadership in a rapidly changing world. The way we interact with technology and each other is on the cusp of a significant shift. Our choices and actions in this era will determine the trajectory of this technological exploration and expansion. Are you ready to navigate the challenges and harness the opportunities of this new era of AI-driven Spatial Computing?

Continued Integration with Daily Life

In the immediate future and the years to come, Spatial Computing and AI will continue to weave themselves into the very essence of our daily lives. This integration will be multifaceted, touching on various aspects of personal and professional spheres.

Here are some of the major ways in which daily life will be affected:

Home and personal environments: In the realm of smart homes, Spatial Computing will enhance the interaction between users and their living spaces. AI-driven virtual assistants will evolve, becoming more intuitive and capable of providing personalized experiences. The use of AR and VR will transform entertainment, allowing for immersive gaming and media consumption experiences that blur the lines between the virtual and real world.

Workplace transformations: The workplace will witness a significant shift with the adoption of these technologies. Spatial Computing, through AR and VR, will revolutionize training and development, allowing employees to engage in lifelike simulations and interactive learning environments. AI will continue to streamline and automate routine tasks, enabling a focus on more creative and strategic activities.

Healthcare advancements: In healthcare, the application of Spatial Computing and AI will lead to improved patient care and innovative treatment methods. Surgeons could use AR for enhanced precision in surgeries, and AI could readily assist in diagnosing diseases more accurately and swiftly, potentially saving lives by identifying conditions early.

Retail and shopping experiences: The retail sector will see a transformation in CXs. Virtual fitting rooms, AR-based product demonstrations, and AI-driven personalized shopping assistants will become commonplace, offering customers a seamless and enhanced shopping experience.

Education and learning: The education sector will benefit greatly from these technologies. Interactive and immersive learning experiences enabled by VR and AR will make education more engaging and accessible. AI's ability to provide personalized learning plans and assessments will revolutionize traditional educational methodologies.

Urban planning and management: In urban development, AI and Spatial Computing will play a crucial role in designing smarter cities. From traffic management to urban planning, these technologies will provide insights and tools to create more efficient and sustainable urban environments.

Transportation and mobility: The future of transportation will be significantly influenced by AI, with autonomous vehicles becoming more prevalent. Spatial Computing will also enhance the navigation and in-vehicle experience, offering interactive and informative displays and controls.

Entertainment and media: The entertainment industry will witness a new era of content creation and consumption. Movies, games, and virtual events will increasingly utilize AR and VR, offering spatial experiences that were once the realm of science fiction.

As we look toward the future, it is clear that Spatial Computing and AI will become deeply embedded in our daily lives, reshaping our experiences and interactions. The next decade promises to be an exciting journey of technological evolution, societal transformation, and endless possibilities.

Enhanced UXs

As we progress into the next decade, the enhancement of UXs through Spatial Computing and AI stands as a pivotal area of development. This evolution will touch virtually every aspect of human interaction with technology, reshaping the way we perceive and engage with the digital world.

Personalization at its core: AI's ability to analyze vast amounts of data and learn from user interactions will drive unprecedented levels of personalization. In areas like entertainment, shopping, and content consumption, this means experiences tailored to individual preferences, habits, and interests. For instance, streaming services could use AI to not only recommend content, but also to adapt it in real time based on user reactions.

Seamless interaction between physical and digital worlds: Spatial Computing will break down the barriers between the physical and digital realms. AR and VR will enable users to interact with digital content in a more natural and intuitive manner. For example, AR overlays in physical environments, like interactive displays in museums or enhanced shopping experiences where digital information is seamlessly integrated into the physical space, will become commonplace.

Revolutionizing entertainment and gaming: The entertainment and gaming industries will undergo a transformative shift. VR and AR will offer immersive experiences that extend beyond screens and devices, creating new forms of storytelling and interactive gaming. Imagine live concerts where the audience, through VR, feels as if it is on stage with the performers, or AR games that transform entire cities into playgrounds.

Advancements in education and training: In education and training, enhanced UXs will facilitate more effective learning. VR and AR can create realistic simulations for training in fields like medicine, aviation, and engineering, offering hands-on experience without the risks associated with real-life training. AI will further enhance this by adapting training modules based on individual learning speeds and styles.

Smarter healthcare interfaces: In healthcare, patient interaction with medical devices and services will be revolutionized. AR could assist in explaining complex medical conditions to patients through 3D visualizations, and AI can provide personalized health recommendations based on individual health data.

Interactive public services and spaces: Public services and spaces will become more interactive and user-friendly. Spatial Computing can be used to enhance navigation in public spaces, like airports or city centers, with AR providing real-time, context-aware information. AI can also be utilized in public service delivery, offering more efficient and tailored services to citizens.

Enhanced accessibility for diverse needs: A significant impact of these technologies will be in making technology more accessible to people with different needs. AI and Spatial Computing can provide customized interfaces and interactions for individuals with disabilities, improving their ability to access and use various services and products.

Workplace productivity and collaboration: In the workplace, these technologies will enhance productivity and collaboration. AR and VR can enable more effective remote collaboration, creating virtual workspaces that mimic physical offices. AI will assist in managing and optimizing workflows, helping employees focus on creative and strategic tasks by automating routine processes.

In essence, the enhancement of UXs through Spatial Computing and AI in the coming decade promises a more intuitive, personalized, and immersive interaction with technology. This evolution will not only redefine entertainment and leisure, but also extend to more practical domains like education, healthcare, public services, and the workplace, fundamentally changing how we live, learn, and work.

Transformative Applications

In the next decade, Spatial Computing and AI are poised to introduce transformative applications that will redefine industries, create new markets, and revolutionize everyday experiences. These applications will not only push the boundaries of what is technologically possible, but also reshape societal norms and business models.

Autonomous systems and robotics: The integration of AI and Spatial Computing will lead to significant advancements in autonomous systems and robotics. We can expect to see more sophisticated autonomous vehicles, drones, and robotic systems capable of navigating and interacting with the physical world with unprecedented precision and intelligence. This will impact sectors like transportation, logistics, agriculture, and manufacturing.

Healthcare revolution: In healthcare, these technologies will enable breakthroughs in diagnostics, treatment planning, and patient care. AI's ability to analyze medical data will lead to more accurate and early disease detection. Spatial Computing, particularly through AR and VR, will be used for surgical simulations, patient education, and even in actual surgeries to guide precision.

Smart cities and urban planning: Spatial Computing and AI will play a critical role in the development of smart cities. These technologies will enable more efficient city planning, traffic management, and resource allocation. AI-driven analysis of urban data can lead to safer, cleaner, and more sustainable living environments.

Advanced manufacturing and supply chain management: In manufacturing and supply chain management, the combination of AI and Spatial Computing will enable more efficient and flexible production processes. AI can optimize supply chains, predict maintenance needs, and enhance quality control. AR can assist workers with complex assembly tasks or provide real-time data overlays in logistics operations.

Revolutionized retail and customer service: Retail and customer service will see a transformation with virtual showrooms, AR-enhanced product visualizations, and AI-driven customer insights. These technologies can create personalized shopping experiences, both online and in physical stores, and enhance customer satisfaction through improved service and interaction.

Evolution of content creation and media: The media and content creation industries will be revolutionized by Spatial Computing and AI. We can expect more personalized and immersive content, like AI-generated music or news, and AR/VR experiences that offer new forms of storytelling and entertainment.

Education and skill development: In education, these technologies will create more immersive and personalized learning experiences. AI can tailor educational content to individual learning styles, while AR and VR can simulate real-world environments for practical learning experiences in fields like history, science, and art.

Environmental monitoring and sustainability: AI and Spatial Computing will play a significant role in environmental monitoring and promoting sustainability. AI can analyze environmental data to predict and mitigate natural disasters, while Spatial Computing can help visualize environmental changes and impact, aiding in education and policymaking.

Enhanced security and surveillance: The application of these technologies in security and surveillance will lead to more sophisticated and effective systems. AI can analyze data from various sources for threat detection and response, while Spatial Computing can provide advanced monitoring capabilities.

Innovative financial services: In the financial sector, AI and Spatial Computing will introduce new ways of customer interaction and service delivery. From AI-driven investment advice to AR-enhanced banking experiences, these technologies will make financial services more accessible and personalized.

The transformative applications of Spatial Computing and AI in the next decade will touch every aspect of our lives, from how we work and learn to how we manage our health and interact with our environment. These developments promise not only technological advancement, but also the potential for significant social and economic impacts, driving innovation and progress across diverse sectors.

Ethical and Regulatory Developments

As we move into the next decade, the landscape of Spatial Computing and AI will be significantly shaped by evolving ethical considerations and regulatory frameworks. While we have thoroughly discussed the nature of the issues confronting us in the previous chapter on ethical and legal issues, the following are the developments currently underway to mitigate these concerns. These new developments will be crucial in guiding the responsible use of these technologies, ensuring they benefit society while mitigating potential risks and negative impacts.

Stricter data privacy and security regulations: The increasing use of AI and Spatial Computing will necessitate stricter data privacy and security regulations. Governments and regulatory bodies will likely introduce more comprehensive laws to protect personal data, similar to the General Data Protection Regulation (GDPR) in the European Union. These regulations will mandate greater transparency and control for users over their data, and stricter penalties for data breaches.

Standards for ethical AI: As AI systems become more prevalent, there will be a growing focus on ethical AI development. This includes creating standards and guidelines to prevent biases in AI algorithms, ensure fairness, and maintain transparency in AI decision-making processes. Ethical considerations will become a core aspect of AI development, with organizations expected to demonstrate their commitment to responsible AI practices.

Regulation of autonomous systems: The rise of autonomous vehicles, drones, and other AI-driven systems will lead to new regulations governing their use. These regulations will address safety standards, liability issues, and ethical concerns, such as decision-making in critical situations. The aim will be to ensure the safe integration of these systems into everyday life, from roads to airspace.

Intellectual property and AI: The next decade will also see developments in intellectual property laws as they relate to AI. Questions around the ownership of AI-generated content and inventions will become more prominent. Lawmakers will grapple with issues, such as whether

AI systems can be considered inventors or authors, and how intellectual property rights are allocated in AI collaborations.

Global standards and collaboration: Given the international nature of technology development and deployment, there will be efforts toward global standards and collaborative frameworks for AI and Spatial Computing. This approach will seek to harmonize regulations across borders, facilitating international cooperation and reducing conflicts between different regulatory regimes.

Focus on sustainability and environmental impact: Ethical and regulatory developments will also encompass the sustainability and environmental impact of these technologies. This might include regulations on the energy consumption of data centers powering AI computations and the environmental footprint of manufacturing and disposing of hardware used in Spatial Computing.

Regulating AI in critical sectors: Specific regulations will emerge for the use of AI in critical sectors like healthcare, finance, and defense. These regulations will ensure that AI applications in these areas are safe, reliable, and do not pose undue risks to public welfare or security.

Public engagement and policy development: There will be a greater emphasis on public engagement in the development of policies and regulations for AI and Spatial Computing. This will involve gathering input from a wide range of stakeholders, including technologists, ethicists, end users, and the general public, to ensure that policies reflect a broad range of interests and concerns.

Adapting education and workforce training: Ethical and regulatory changes will also drive adaptations in education and workforce training. As new standards and laws are implemented, professionals working with these technologies will need to be educated on ethical considerations, compliance requirements, and best practices.

Ethical and regulatory developments in the realm of Spatial Computing and AI will play a critical role in shaping the future of these technologies. By addressing key issues around privacy, security, ethical development, and sustainability, these developments will ensure that the advancements in Spatial Computing and AI are aligned with societal values and contribute positively to human progress.

Collaboration and Connectivity

As we advance into the next decade, collaboration and connectivity will emerge as fundamental themes in the evolution of Spatial Computing and AI. These technologies will not only enhance how individuals and organizations connect and work together, but also foster new types of collaboration and create deeper levels of interconnectedness.

Enhanced remote collaboration: Spatial Computing, especially through AR and VR, will revolutionize remote collaboration. Virtual workspaces that mimic physical offices will become more common, enabling teams spread across the globe to interact as if they were in the same room. This will include virtual meetings, where participants can interact with 3D models or data in real-time, enhancing both engagement and productivity.

AI-powered communication tools: AI will play a significant role in enhancing communication tools, making them more efficient and intuitive. Natural language processing and ML will enable more sophisticated virtual assistants and chatbots that can facilitate communication, manage schedules, and even predict and prepare for future collaboration needs.

Interoperability and standardization: As Spatial Computing and AI technologies mature, there will be a greater emphasis on interoperability and standardization. This will facilitate seamless integration across different platforms and devices, ensuring that collaboration tools can work together without technical barriers. It will also involve developing common standards for data formats and communication protocols.

Social connectivity through AR and VR: AR and VR will transform social interactions by creating more immersive and interactive ways to connect. This might include virtual social spaces where people can meet and interact in a more lifelike manner, transcending geographical boundaries. These technologies will also offer new avenues for cultural experiences, such as virtual tours of museums or historical sites.

Collaborative AI development: The development of AI itself will become more collaborative. Open-source platforms and crowd-sourced data will become increasingly important, allowing for a more diverse range of inputs and perspectives in AI development. This collaborative approach will help in creating more robust and unbiased AI systems.

Connectivity in smart cities: Spatial Computing and AI will enhance connectivity in smart cities, linking various services and infrastructure for more efficient urban management. This includes integrating transportation systems, public services, and utilities into a cohesive network, all managed through advanced AI algorithms for optimal performance.

Enhanced customer interaction: In retail and customer service, these technologies will enable more personalized and interactive CXs. For example, AI can analyze customer data to provide tailored recommendations, while AR can be used for virtual product demonstrations, enhancing the customer's decision-making process.

Collaboration in healthcare: In healthcare, Spatial Computing and AI will enable new levels of collaboration among healthcare professionals.

For example, specialists from different parts of the world could collaborate in real-time on complex surgeries using AR, or share insights on patient treatment plans assisted by AI analytics.

Educational collaboration and learning networks: In education, these technologies will foster collaborative learning environments and global learning networks. Students from different parts of the world could participate in virtual classrooms, engage in collaborative projects, and share resources, all enhanced by AI-driven personalized learning experiences.

In summary, the future of Spatial Computing and AI is intrinsically linked to enhanced collaboration and connectivity. These technologies will not only improve existing methods of collaboration, but also create new paradigms of interconnectedness, bringing together people, data, and systems in ways that were previously unimaginable. This enhanced connectivity will drive innovation, improve efficiency, and foster a sense of global community across various sectors and aspects of life.

Cultural and Social Impacts

As we look toward the next decade, the cultural and social impacts of Spatial Computing and AI will become increasingly prominent. These technologies are set to redefine our societal norms, influence cultural developments, and shape human interactions in profound ways.

Redefining human interaction and communication: Spatial Computing, particularly through AR and VR, will transform how we interact and communicate with each other. Virtual environments will offer new spaces for social interaction, transcending physical limitations and allowing people to connect in more immersive and engaging ways. This could lead to the formation of new types of online communities and social networks based on shared virtual experiences.

Impact on art and creativity: Art and creativity will see significant transformations. Artists and creators will have new tools at their disposal, enabling them to craft experiences that blend the physical and digital worlds. AI will also emerge as a creative partner, offering new ways to generate art, music, and literature, potentially challenging our traditional notions of creativity and artistic authorship.

Changes in consumer behavior and expectations: As consumers become more accustomed to personalized and immersive experiences enabled by Spatial Computing and AI, their expectations and behaviors will evolve. Businesses will need to adapt to these changing demands, offering more tailored and engaging experiences, both online and in physical spaces.

Educational transformation: Education will become more accessible and personalized. Virtual and augmented classrooms will break down geographical barriers, enabling students from different parts of the world to learn together. AI's ability to tailor educational content to individual learning styles will make education more effective and inclusive.

Influence on mental health and wellness: The integration of Spatial Computing and AI in mental health and wellness will offer new forms of therapy and self-care. VR, for instance, can be used for immersive therapy sessions, providing safe environments for patients to explore difficult experiences or phobias. AI-driven apps can offer personalized mental health advice and support.

Ethical and societal challenges: The widespread adoption of these technologies will also raise ethical and societal challenges. Issues such as digital divide, privacy concerns, and the potential for AI and AR/VR to be used in manipulative or harmful ways will require careful consideration and proactive management.

Cultural preservation and dissemination: Spatial Computing and AI will play a role in cultural preservation and dissemination. VR can bring historical sites and cultural experiences to a broader audience, making them more accessible and aiding in their preservation. AI can help in analyzing and understanding cultural artifacts, offering new insights into our history and heritage.

Work-life balance and lifestyle changes: The integration of these technologies into the workplace and homes will also impact work-life balance and lifestyles. Remote working and virtual offices may become more prevalent, offering flexibility, but also blurring the lines between personal and professional life.

Globalization and cross-cultural exchange: Spatial Computing and AI will further enhance globalization, promoting cross-cultural exchange and understanding. Virtual environments can facilitate interactions and collaborations among individuals from diverse cultural backgrounds, promoting a more inclusive and connected world.

The cultural and social impacts of Spatial Computing and AI over the next decade will be far-reaching. While these technologies offer exciting possibilities for enhancing human experiences, creativity, and global connectivity, they also present new challenges and ethical considerations. Navigating these impacts will require thoughtful engagement from all sectors of society, ensuring that the benefits of these technologies are realized while their potential risks are responsibly managed.

Sustainability and Environmental Considerations

As we progress into the next decade, the role of Spatial Computing and AI in driving sustainability and addressing environmental concerns will become increasingly significant. These technologies have the potential to contribute positively to environmental efforts, but they also pose new challenges that need to be addressed responsibly.

Energy efficiency and resource management: AI will play a crucial role in optimizing energy usage and resource management. By analyzing large sets of environmental data, AI can help in developing more efficient ways to use resources, reduce waste, and lower carbon footprints. In industries like manufacturing and logistics, AI-driven optimizations can lead to significant reductions in energy consumption and emissions.

Environmental monitoring and protection: Spatial Computing and AI will enhance our ability to monitor environmental changes and protect ecosystems. AI algorithms can process data from satellites, sensors, and drones to track environmental phenomena like deforestation, ocean health, and air quality. This data can inform conservation strategies and policy decisions.

Smart and sustainable cities: In urban development, these technologies will contribute to the creation of smart cities that are more sustainable and efficient. AI can be used for intelligent traffic management, reducing congestion and pollution, while Spatial Computing can aid in urban planning by simulating different development scenarios and their environmental impacts.

Climate change analysis and mitigation: AI's ability to analyze complex and vast data sets will be invaluable in studying climate change. It can provide more accurate predictions of climate patterns and extreme weather events, aiding in mitigation and adaptation strategies. AI can also assist in modeling the effectiveness of different climate change countermeasures.

Sustainable agriculture and food production: In agriculture, AI and Spatial Computing can lead to more sustainable practices. AI can help in precision farming, optimizing the use of water, fertilizers, and pesticides, while minimizing environmental impact. Spatial Computing can assist farmers in monitoring crop health and soil conditions, enhancing yield and reducing waste.

Green technology and renewable energy: These technologies will also support the development and deployment of green technology and renewable energy. AI can optimize the operation of renewable energy systems like solar and wind farms, improving their efficiency and integration into the power grid.

Challenges of tech sustainability: However, the sustainability of the technology itself is a concern. The production and operation of AI and Spatial Computing hardware and infrastructure, including data centers, require significant energy, which can contribute to carbon emissions. Addressing the environmental impact of these technologies will be crucial, including efforts to use renewable energy sources and develop more energy-efficient hardware and algorithms.

Lifecycle assessment and circular economy: Lifecycle assessment of technology products will gain importance. This involves evaluating the environmental impact of a product from production to disposal. The concept of a circular economy, where products are designed for reuse and recycling, will be crucial in reducing the environmental footprint of technology.

Public awareness and behavioral change: Last, these technologies can play a role in increasing public awareness about environmental issues and promoting behavioral change. Interactive and immersive experiences created through AR and VR can educate people about the impacts of climate change and environmental degradation, motivating them to adopt more sustainable practices.

Sustainability and environmental considerations will be integral to the development and application of Spatial Computing and AI in the next decade. While these technologies offer powerful tools for environmental management and protection, addressing their own environmental impacts will be essential for a sustainable and responsible technological future.

Conclusions: Embracing AI-Driven Spatial Computing

As we conclude, it's evident that the integration of AI-driven Spatial Computing into our lives is not just a future possibility but an unfolding reality. This technological transformation will reshape our everyday interactions, redefine UXs, and introduce groundbreaking applications in numerous fields. The increasing significance of collaboration and connectivity, coupled with the profound cultural and social impacts, will alter the fabric of human interactions and societal norms. Moreover, addressing sustainability and environmental implications of these technologies is imperative for a balanced and responsible technological future.

We are entering an era where the boundaries between the digital and physical worlds are increasingly blurred, thanks to the advancements in

Spatial Computing and AI. We like to consider it a marriage of two worlds that, together, build an even better world than the one we know. These technologies will become deeply interwoven into the fabric of our daily lives, revolutionizing how we interact with our environment, entertain ourselves, and perform our jobs. The potential for transformative changes spans from our homes to healthcare facilities, and from virtual entertainment platforms to innovative workplace solutions.

The future of UXs is set to be dramatically enhanced by the capabilities of Spatial Computing and AI. This will lead to a more seamless interaction between the physical and digital realms, offering personalized and immersive experiences across various sectors, including entertainment, education, and healthcare. These advancements will fundamentally change our engagement with digital content and interfaces.

The transformative applications of Spatial Computing and AI are poised to redefine existing industries and give rise to new markets. Whether it's through autonomous systems, the development of smart cities, advancements in manufacturing, or breakthroughs in healthcare, these technologies will disrupt traditional practices and introduce novel paradigms.

As we embrace these technological advances, ethical and regulatory developments will play a crucial role. The focus on responsible innovation, data privacy, and adherence to ethical standards will be essential to ensure the beneficial application of these technologies and prevent potential harms.

Enhanced collaboration and connectivity will redefine how individuals and organizations communicate and work together. Innovations in remote collaboration, powered by AR and VR, along with AI-enhanced communication tools, will create more interconnected and efficient work environments. Rather than separating us into separate, solitary worlds, these technological advances will bring us closer together to work much more efficiently.

The cultural and social ramifications of Spatial Computing and AI are expected to be substantial. These technologies will have a significant impact on art, creativity, education, mental health, and wellness. They will transform social interactions and lead to shifts in consumer behaviors and expectations.

Last, the role of Spatial Computing and AI in fostering sustainability and addressing environmental challenges is crucial. While these technologies offer immense opportunities for environmental management and conservation, their ecological footprint must be managed responsibly.

As we navigate this transformative era, it's essential to be conscious of the opportunities and challenges posed by AI-driven Spatial Computing. The future holds immense potential, and our decisions and actions will significantly influence the direction of this technological evolution. The path ahead is set to be transformative, demanding adaptability, ethical mindfulness, and a commitment to sustainable development. Our book has aimed to serve as both a roadmap and a call to action, encouraging us to approach the future with insight, responsibility, and a dedication to leveraging technology for the collective benefit of society.

Notes

Foreword

1. Porter, J. (2023 November 6). ChatGPT continues to be one of the fastest-growing services ever. The Verge. https://www.theverge.com/2023/11/6/23948386/chatgpt-active-user-count-openai-developer-conference#

Introduction

1. Takahashi, Dean. (2019 December 10). Magic Leap formally launches Magic Leap 1 and reveals enterprise partners. VentureBeat. https://venturebeat.com/business/magic-leap-formally-launches-magic-leap-1-and-reveals-enterprise-partners/
2. Vass, B. The best way to predict the future is to simulate it. (2022 September 12). AWS Spatial Computing Blog. https://aws.amazon.com/blogs/spatial/the-best-way-to-predict-the-future-is-to-simulate-it/

Chapter 1

1. Immersive e-commerce accelerated by AI. (n.d.). Obsess. https://obsessar.com/feature-ai-accelerated-virtual-stores/
2. Welch, A. (2023 September 14). Artificial intelligence is helping revolutionize healthcare as we know it. Content Lab U.S. https://www.jnj.com/innovation/artificial-intelligence-in-healthcare
3. John Deere. (2022 January 4). John Deere reveals fully autonomous tractor at CES 2022. www.deere.com. https://www.deere.com/en/news/all-news/autonomous-tractor-reveal/
4. Rogers, J. (2023 September 26). Spatial computing is the next frontier in airline flight safety. IBM Blog. https://www.ibm.com/blog/spatial-computing-is-the-next-frontier-in-airline-flight-safety/
5. Sketch, G. (2020 April 8). Enterprise use Cases for spatial computing. Gravity Sketch. https://www.gravitysketch.com/blog/articles/enterprise-use-cases-for-spatial-computing
6. Tomilli. (2023 March 9). Action Audio's NBA debut. Tomilli. https://tomilli.com/usa-canada-action-audios-nba-debut/
7. Lemire, J. (2023 July 13). How the NBA is testing Hawk-Eye's tracking and video replay system to help refs. www.sportsbusinessjournal.com. https://www.sportsbusinessjournal.com/Journal/Issues/2023/07/10/Technology/nba-hawkeye.aspx

Chapter 2

1. Takahashi, Dean. (10 December 2019). Magic Leap formally launches Magic Leap 1 and reveals enterprise partners. VentureBeat. venturebeat.com/business/magic-leap-formally-launches-magic-leap-1-and-reveals-enterprise-partners/

2. Lee, C. (2023 May 23). Exploring the spatial computing spectrum: The next frontier of immersive technologies. AWS Spatial Computing Blog. https://aws.amazon.com/blogs/spatial/exploring-the-spatial-computing-spectrum-the-next-frontier-of-immersive-technologies/

3. Vass, B. (2022 September 12). The best way to predict the future is to simulate it. AWS Spatial Computing Blog. https://aws.amazon.com/blogs/spatial/the-best-way-to-predict-the-future-is-to-simulate-it/

4. Funnell, R. (2022 November 22). Can a circle of salt paralyze a self-driving car? IFLScience. https://www.iflscience.com/can-a-circle-of-salt-paralyze-a-self-driving-car-66313

5. Christian, K. (2021 September 21). Drone delivery services halted as birds and machines clash in Canberra's air space. ABC News. https://www.abc.net.au/news/2021-09-22/territorial-ravens-disrupt-canberra-drone-deliveries/100480470

6. Bavor, C. (2021 May 18). Project Starline: Feel like you're there, together. Google. https://blog.google/technology/research/project-starline/

7. BNP Paribas rolls out world premiere teleportation meetings with Magic Leap & Mimesys—BNP Paribas. (2019). BNP Paribas. https://group.bnpparibas/en/press-release/bnp-paribas-rolls-world-premiere-teleportation-meetings-magic-leap-mimesys

8. Forbes: Five Enterprise XR lessons from Lockheed. (n.d.). Scope AR. https://www.scopear.com/news/forbes-five-enterprise-xr-lessons-from-lockheed

9. A spatial computing case study: Jabil and Magic Leap. (n.d.). https://www.jabil.com/blog/spatial-computing-case-study.html

10. Dahlberg, N. (2019 October 22). How technology is helping those on the autism spectrum master the job interview. Miamiherald.com. https://www.miamiherald.com/living/helping-others/article236501368.html

11. Stojanovic, M. (2021 November 2). Gamer demographics from 2023: No longer a men-only club. https://playtoday.co/blog/stats/gamer-demographics

12. Jane McGonigal, *Reality Is Broken Why Games Make Us Better and How They Can Change the World*, Penguin Books, p. 126.

13. Statt, N. (2020 May 14). Apple confirms it bought virtual reality event startup NextVR. The Verge. https://www.theverge.com/2020/5/14/21211254/apple-confirms-nextvr-acquisition-purchase-vr-virtual-reality-company

14. GoT: The dead must die. (n.d.). World.magicleap.com. https://world.magicleap.com/en-us/details/com.magicleap.deadmustdie

Chapter 4

1. Andy Wilson at Microsoft Research. (n.d.). Microsoft Research. Retrieved January 11, 2024, from https://www.microsoft.com/en-us/research/people/awilson/projects/

2. DreamWalker: Substituting real-world walking experiences with a virtual reality. (2019 October 21). Microsoft Research. https://www.microsoft.com/en-us/research/video/dreamwalker-substituting-real-world-walking-experiences-with-a-virtual-reality-2/

3. Panda, P., Nicholas, M. J., Nguyen, D., Ofek, E., Pahud, M., Rintel, S., Franco, M. G., Hinckley, K., and Lanier, J. (2023 July 1). Beyond audio: Towards a design space of headphones as a site for interaction and sensing. www.microsoft.com. https://www.microsoft.com/en-us/research/publication/beyond-audio-towards-a-design-space-of-headphones-as-a-site-for-interaction-and-sensing/

4. Amazon Web Services. (2022 December 2). AWS re:Invent 2022—Keynote with Dr. Werner Vogels. YouTube. https://www.youtube.com/watch?v=RfvL_423a-I&t=4320s

5. Jackson II, D., and Richards, K. (2023 October 23). Getting started with Vision Pro and AWS. AWS Spatial Computing Blog. https://aws.amazon.com/blogs/spatial/getting-started-with-vision-pro-and-aws/

6. Dresser, S. (2023 October 18). Amazon announces 2 new ways it's using robots to assist employees and deliver for customers. About Amazon. https://www.aboutamazon.com/news/operations/amazon-introduces-new-robotics-solutions

7. Amazon. (2022 June 21). Look back on 10 years of Amazon robotics. About Amazon. https://www.aboutamazon.com/news/operations/10-years-of-amazon-robotics-how-robots-help-sort-packages-move-product-and-improve-safety

8. Robotics Software Engineer, Autonomous Systems—SPG—Careers at Apple. (2022 September 16). https://jobs.apple.com/en-us/details/200425943/robotics-software-engineer-autonomous-systems-spg

9. Ego How-To—Research—AI at Meta. (n.d.). https://ai.meta.com/research/ego-how-to/

10. Argyle. (n.d.). www.argyle.build. Retrieved January 11, 2024, from https://www.argyle.build/

11. How Vuforia step check improves quality with AI. (2023 May 10). PTC. https://www.ptc.com/en/resources/digital-download/vuforia-step-check-improving-quality-with-ai-enhanced-visual-inspection

12. Lauren Kunze. (n.d.). ICONIQ AI. LinkedIn. www.linkedin.com. https://www.linkedin.com/in/lkunze/

13. Kuki. (n.d.). Chat with me! Chat.kuki.ai. https://chat.kuki.ai/chat

14. About. (n.d.). @Kuki_ai. https://www.kuki.ai/about

15. Kuki_ai. Cathy Hackl talks to her Metabot "Niko." (2021 December 16). YouTube. https://www.youtube.com/watch?v=4G9RWjrlVSM

16. Home Page. (n.d.). Sanctuary.ai. https://sanctuary.ai/

17. Hackl, C. (n.d.). Everything you ever wanted to know about synthetic humanoid robots or synths. *Forbes*. Retrieved January 11, 2024, from https://www.forbes.com/sites/cathyhackl/2020/07/05/everything-you-ever-wanted-to-know-about-synthetic-humanoid-robots-or-synths/

18. Tesla. (2023). Artificial intelligence & autopilot. Tesla. www.tesla.com. https://www.tesla.com/AI

19. @Tesla. (2023 February 13). X.com. https://x.com/Tesla/status/16252222499920363 54?s=20

20. How Deere & Company is embracing AI and putting the technology in the hands of farmers. (2023 September 6). Wqad.com. https://www.wqad.com/article/news/agriculture/how-deere-company-is-embracing-ai-and-putting-the-technology-in-the-hands-of-farmers-good-morning-quad-cities-east-moline-john-deere/526-c168e9e0-ec53-496e-99a5-e89dd2c627fb
21. Innovation award honorees. (n.d.). www.ces.tech. https://www.ces.tech/innovation-awards/honorees/2023/best-of/j/john-deere-autonomous-tractor.aspx
22. Metaphysic.ai—Hyperreal content made with AI. (n.d.). https://Metaphysic.ai/. https://metaphysic.ai/
23. Giardina, C. (2023 January 31). Tom Hanks, Robin Wright to be de-aged in Robert Zemeckis' new movie using metaphysic AI tool. The Hollywood Reporter. https://www.hollywoodreporter.com/movies/movie-news/metaphysic-ai-tom-hanks-robin-wright-deaged-robert-zemeckis-caa-1235313318/
24. Wonder Dynamics. (n.d.). https://wonderdynamics.com
25. Leadership development. (n.d.). Talespin. Retrieved January 11, 2024, from https://www.talespin.com/leadership-development
26. Talespin. Where'd everybody go? The business leader's guide to the decentralized workforce. (2023 February 9). YouTube. https://www.youtube.com/watch?v=nSAKz0GXNHw&t=2s
27. CoPilot designer—AI-powered no-code content authoring tool. (n.d.). www.talespin.com. Retrieved January 11, 2024, from https://www.talespin.com/copilot-designer?utm_source=screenspace&utm_content=lp1
28. The invisible computing company. (n.d.). Mojo Vision. https://www.mojo.vision/
29. The Mojo Blog: A new direction. (n.d.). Mojo Vision. https://www.mojo.vision/news/a-new-direction

Chapter 5

1. Howell, E. (2017 January 24). NASA's real "Hidden Figures." Space.com. https://www.space.com/35430-real-hidden-figures.html
2. Ellingrud, K., Sanghvi, S., Singh Dandona, G., Madgavkar, A., Chui, M., White, O., and Hasebe, P. (2023 July 26). Generative AI and the future of work in America | McKinsey. www.mckinsey.com. https://www.mckinsey.com/mgi/our-research/generative-ai-and-the-future-of-work-in-america
3. Professional Certificate in Foresight | Technology Division at the Cullen College of Engineering. (n.d.). Dot.egr.uh.edu. https://dot.egr.uh.edu/programs/professional/fore
4. Klemp, N. (2019 November 14). Google encourages employees to take time off to be creative: Here's how you can too, without sacrificing outcomes. Inc.com. https://www.inc.com/nate-klemp/google-encourages-employees-to-take-time-off-to-be-creative-heres-how-you-can-too-without-sacrificing-outcomes.html
5. Tamayo, J., Doumi, L., Goel, S., Kovács-Ondrejkovic, O., and Sadun, R. (2023 September 1). Reskilling in the age of AI. Harvard Business Review. https://hbr.org/2023/09/reskilling-in-the-age-of-ai
6. IDC Data Growth Predictions. (n.d.). Virstor. Retrieved January 22, 2024, from https://virstor.co.uk/idc-data-growth-predictions

7. O'Halloran, J. (2023 October 26). Nimo Planet completes spatial computing system for hybrid work [Review of Nimo Planet completes spatial computing system for hybrid work]. ComputerWeekly.com. https://www.computerweekly.com/news/366557215/Nimo-Planet-completes-spatial-computing-system-for-hybrid-work

8. Fortune Editors. (2023, November 1). *L'Oréal CEO explains why the 114-year-old beauty company spends a billion euro a year on tech—more than it invests in R&D* (Fortune Editors, Ed.) [Review of *L'Oréal CEO explains why the 114-year-old beauty company spends a billion euro a year on tech—more than it invests in R&D*]. Yahoo! Finance. https://finance.yahoo.com/news/l-al-ceo-explains-why-200003978.html

9. Esposito, A. (2023 June 7). Sensory enabling technologies are radically reshaping the future of digital retail. Retail TouchPoints. https://www.retailtouchpoints.com/topics/retail-innovation/sensory-enabling-technologies-digital-retail

Chapter 6

1. Adobe Experience Cloud Team. (2023 August 10). Customer experience—what it is, why it's important, and how to deliver it. Adobe Experience Cloud. https://business.adobe.com/blog/basics/customer-experience

2. Adobe Experience Cloud Team. (2021 August 19). User Experience (UX). Adobe Experience Cloud. https://business.adobe.com/blog/basics/user-experience

3. TechMagic. (n.d.). Adweek. https://www.adweek.com/podcasts/tech-magic/

4. Nast, C. (2023 December 12). "Gamified" virtual stores target new generation of consumer. Vogue Business. https://www.voguebusiness.com/story/technology/gamified-virtual-stores-target-new-generation-of-consumer

5. Deloitte. (2023). While we wait for the metaverse to materialize, young people are already there. Deloitte Insights. https://www.deloitte.com/us/en/insights/industry/technology/gen-z-and-millennials-are-metaverse-early-adopters.html

6. Hackl, C. (2023 November 29). TechMagic Podcast: Lego x Fortnite and the god-mothers of AI. Adweek. https://www.adweek.com/media/techmagic-podcast-lego-x-fortnite-and-the-godmothers-of-ai/

About the Authors

Cathy Hackl

Cathy Hackl (@cathyhackl) is a globally recognized tech and gaming executive, futurist, author, and keynote speaker who focuses on Spatial Computing, virtual worlds, Augmented Reality (AR), Artificial Intelligence (AI), tech trends, strategic foresight, and gaming platforms strategy.

She's one of the top technology voices on LinkedIn and is the host of Adweek's *TechMagic* podcast. Cathy has worked at Amazon Web Services, Magic Leap, and HTC VIVE, and has advised companies such as Nike, Ralph Lauren, Walmart, Louis Vuitton, and Clinique on their emerging tech journeys. As a sought-after keynote speaker, she has spoken at Harvard Business School, MIT, SXSW, Comic-Con, World Economic Forum Annual Meeting in Davos 2023, Consumer Electronic show (CES), Mobile World Congress (MWC), *Vogue*'s Forces of Fashion, and more. She has been recognized as one of Ad Age's Leading Women of 2023, *Bloomberg Linea*'s 100 Top Innovators, and *Newsweek*'s top Latina women working in AI. She was featured on the cover of *Forbes Centroamérica*'s 100 Most Powerful Women 2023 issue and is on the *Vogue Business* 100 Innovators list.

Popularly known in tech circles as the "Godmother of the Metaverse" and one of the world's leading tech futurists, Cathy has been a major player in the world of immersive technology for almost a decade with numerous media appearances in CNBC's *Squawk Box, 60 Minutes*, CNN, *Good Morning America, GQ, Time, Wall Street Journal, Washington Post, The Economist*, Bloomberg, and is a guest editor for *Vogue Singapore*. In 2022, she became the first human—in physical *and* avatar form—to ring NASDAQ's opening bell and open the financial markets on live television. She's taught at IE Business School and SDA Bocconi School of Management, and holds bylines at the *Harvard Business Review, Wired, Forbes*, and *Fast Company*.

Irena Cronin

Irena Cronin is Senior Vice President of Product for DADOS Technology, which is creating a data analytics and visualization platform for the Apple Vision Pro. She is also the CEO of Infinite Retina, which provides research to help companies develop and implement Artificial Intelligence (AI), Augmented Reality (AR), and other new technologies for their businesses. Previous to this, she worked for several years as an equity research analyst and gained extensive experience in evaluating both public and private companies.

Irena has a joint MBA/MA from the University of Southern California and an MS with Distinction in Management and Systems from New York University. She graduated with a BA from the University of Pennsylvania with a major in economics (summa cum laude). She has near-fluent proficiency in Mandarin; intermediate, in Japanese; and beginning, in Korean.

Acknowledgments

Both authors wish to thank Jeanenne Ray, Casper Barbour, and the rest of the team at Wiley Business.

Irena Cronin especially wants to thank Carol Cox, her best friend, who made sure that she did other things besides writing and working that ultimately made everything better, and her brother, Alex Kaluti, for his kindness. Irena also wants to thank her co-writer Cathy Hackl for the joy in writing this book, and David Chalmers, Peter Coolidge, Marylene Delbourg-Delphis, Ken Gardner, Luke Gardner, Jon Malysiak, Matt Miesnieks, Elon Musk, Jeremiah Owyang, Matt Rastovac, Philip Rosedale, Jason Schneiderman, Robert Scoble, Steve Sinclair, Brian Solis, Nick St. Pierre, Chris Stokel-Walker, Hugo Swart, Mojtaba Tabatabaie, Dean Takahashi, and Dilmer Valecillos.

Cathy Hackl wants to thank Irena Cronin for partnering on this book. Cathy also wants to thank her family and her children for all their support during a year of many changes in their lives. She also wants to acknowledge the following people: Sacha Knopp, Faith Popcorn, Monica Vallin, Susanne Mathieu, Leslie Shannon, Lindsey McInerney, Andrew Schwartz, Lee Kebler, Charlotte Perman, Sonya Denyse, Lily Snyder, John Buzzell, Isidora de Vicente, Ignacio Acosta, Alberto Carrillo, Jessica Matack, Glenda Umana, Emile Hoffman, Iraida Rivas, Charlie Fink, Rafaella Camera, Cortney Harding, Joanna Popper, Tom Emrich, Richard Entrup, Marni Puente, Kathleen Hessert, Rani Mani, Leah Nathan, Deb Greyson Riegel, Allie K. Miller, Susan Higginbotham, Sarah and KC Blake, Samantha Wolfe, Greg Kahn, Tina Tuli, Tony Parisi, Rony Abovitz, Ted Schilowitz, Anifa Mvuemba, Karyn Gorman, Charissa Cheong, David Bundi, the IoDF crew, Marjorie Hernandez, Amy Peck, Roger Spitz, Gary Vee, Avery Akkineni, Andrea Sullivan, Eric Redmond, and UTA, Adweek's Podcast Network, the Association of Professional Futurists, and the Female Quotient.

Index